W9-AYD-450

LIBRARY OF
CONGRESS
SURPLUS
DUPLICATE
NOT FOR RESALE

Other books in the People in the News series:

Tim Tebow

By Jenny MacKay

LUCENT BOOKS
A part of Gale, Cengage Learning

GALE
CENGAGE Learning·

Detroit • New York • San Francisco • New Haven, Conn • Waterville, Maine • London

Lanham Christian School
8400 Good Luck Rd.
Lanham, MD 20706

© 2013 Gale, Cengage Learning

ALL RIGHTS RESERVED. No part of this work covered by the copyright herein may be repro-
duced, transmitted, stored, or used in any form or by any means graphic, electronic, or
mechanical, including but not limited to photocopying, recording, scanning, digitizing, taping,
Web distribution, information networks, or information storage and retrieval systems, except
as permitted under Section 107 or 108 of the 1976 United States Copyright Act, without the
prior written permission of the publisher.

Every effort has been made to trace the owners of copyrighted material.

Library of Congress Cataloging-in-Publication Data

Mackay, Jenny.
Tim Tebow / by Jenny MacKay.
    pages cm. -- (People in the news)
Includes bibliographical references and index.
ISBN 978-1-4205-0893-2 (hardcover)
1. Tebow, Tim, 1987---Juvenile literature 2. Football players--United States--Biography--
Juvenile literature. 3. Quarterbacks (Football)--United States--Biography--Juvenile
literature. I. Title.
GV939.T423M335 2013
796.332092--dc23
[B]
                                                                        2012049994

Lucent Books
27500 Drake Rd
Farmington Hills MI 48331

ISBN-13: 978-1-4205-0893-2
ISBN-10: 1-4205-0893-8

Printed in the United States of America
1 2 3 4 5 6 7 17 16 15 14 13

Contents

Fame and celebrity are alluring. People are drawn to those who walk in fame's spotlight, whether they are known for great accomplishments or for notorious deeds. The lives of the famous pique public interest and attract attention, perhaps because their experiences seem in some ways so different from, yet in other ways so similar to, our own.

Newspapers, magazines, and television regularly capitalize on this fascination with celebrity by running profiles of famous people. For example, television programs such as *Entertainment Tonight* devote all their programming to stories about entertainment and entertainers. Magazines such as *People* fill their pages with stories of the private lives of famous people. Even newspapers, newsmagazines, and television news frequently delve into the lives of well-known personalities. Despite the number of articles and programs, few provide more than a superficial glimpse at their subjects.

Lucent's People in the News series offers young readers a deeper look into the lives of today's newsmakers, the influences that have shaped them, and the impact they have had in their fields of endeavor and on other people's lives. The subjects of the series hail from many disciplines and walks of life. They include authors, musicians, athletes, political leaders, entertainers, entrepreneurs, and others who have made a mark on modern life and who, in many cases, will continue to do so for years to come.

These biographies are more than factual chronicles. Each book emphasizes the contributions, accomplishments, or deeds that have brought fame or notoriety to the individual and shows how that person has influenced modern life. Authors portray their subjects in a realistic, unsentimental light. For example, Bill Gates—cofounder of the software giant Microsoft—has been instrumental in making personal computers the most vital tool of the modern age. Few dispute his business savvy, his perseverance, or his technical expertise, yet critics say he is ruthless in his dealings with competitors and driven more by his desire to maintain Microsoft's dominance in the computer industry than by an interest in furthering technology.

In these books, young readers will encounter inspiring stories about real people who achieved success despite enormous obstacles. Oprah Winfrey—one of the most powerful, most watched, and wealthiest women in television history—spent the first six years of her life in the care of her grandparents while her unwed mother sought work and a better life elsewhere. Her adolescence was colored by pregnancy at age fourteen, rape, and sexual abuse.

Each author documents and supports his or her work with an array of primary and secondary source quotations taken from diaries, letters, speeches, and interviews. All quotes are footnoted to show readers exactly how and where biographers derive their information and provide guidance for further research. The quotations enliven the text by giving readers eyewitness views of the life and accomplishments of each person covered in the People in the News series.

In addition, each book in the series includes photographs, annotated bibliographies, timelines, and comprehensive indexes. For both the casual reader and the student researcher, the People in the News series offers insight into the lives of today's newsmakers—people who shape the way we live, work, and play in the modern age.

A Football Phenom

Tim Tebow is a professional football player. He started playing in Pop Warner football programs as a kid, and when he reached high school, he joined the football team, helping them win a state championship. At the University of Florida, he played quarterback for the Gators, leading the team to two national college football titles. Tebow's performance with the Gators earned him numerous awards, including the prestigious Heisman Trophy, an annual award presented to just one college football player for excellence. After graduating from college, Tebow became a professional football player, first joining the Denver Broncos and then the New York Jets.

A Controversial Quarterback

The youngest of five children, Tebow grew up in a religious family; his parents were evangelical missionaries. The Tebows lived on a farm in Florida, where Tebow and his two older brothers played football together. These family football games taught Tebow to be relentlessly competitive, and later, when he was a star quarterback in high school, he learned to be humble.

While Tebow has found success as a football player, there are people who criticize, ridicule, and even mock his playing style, his religion, and his political beliefs. He has been the butt of jokes told by late-night talk-show hosts and the subject of skits on the late-night television show, *Saturday Night Live*. He is routinely lambasted for his lack of passing finesse. He also has a playing

Tim Tebow has had a profound effect on the sports world, as well as popular culture. He is known as much for his strong faith as for his athletic prowess. This nine-year-old Tebow fan wears eye black with a biblical reference, for which Tebow became famous.

style that forces coaches to craft unusual game plans that work around his quirky habits and methods. Tebow's critics chalk up his successes to the hard work of his teammates; they scoff at the notion that he does anything spectacular to win games.

Some of Tebow's most avid fans claim a higher power is responsible for the quarterback's stardom. His critics, however, are quick to say that luck and coincidence have been misread as the power of God at work on the field. Tebow himself has never suggested that God helps him win football games, yet many interpret the link between his religious displays and the improbable wins he pulls off as signs of divine intervention. Amid all the hype, Tebow continues to pray and play.

Tebow's persona is the subject of many jokes in popular culture. Comedian Jimmy Fallon created a character based on David Bowie and Tim Tebow, known as Tebowie. The comedic skit consisted of a musical conversation between Tebow and God.

A Player with a Conscience

Tebow is most visible to the public when he is on a football field, but when fewer cameras are watching, he is visiting orphans, death-row inmates, or children who are hospitalized for life-threatening illnesses. He once pushed a wheelchair-bound teenager around a football field before a college game. He took a ten-year-old girl with a serious autoimmune disease on a date to the Cartoon Network Hall of Game Awards. He also sends personalized Christmas gifts to people with disabilities who he met during the year. He vows to never be seen smoking or drinking alcohol in public, in case young people are watching. He is also open about the fact that he is waiting until he is married to have sex, which sets him apart from many of his peers who are known for being sexually promiscuous.

Tebow's charisma, as well as his football talent, has made him one of the most recognizable athletes in America and earned him numerous distinctions, including being listed as number two on *Forbes* magazine's 2012 list of the most influential athletes in America, second only to race-car driver Jimmie Johnson.

Chapter 1

Growing Up Gifted

Tim Tebow was born to Americans Bob and Pam Tebow on August 14, 1987, in the city of Manila in the Republic of the Philippines. The Tebows consider Tim's birth to be a God-given miracle because Pam had serious complications during the pregnancy. In the end, though, Tim grew into a healthy, normal boy and gifted football player.

An Uncertain Pregnancy

In 1985 Bob and Pam, who were Christian Baptist missionaries, sold most of their belongings and moved from Florida to the Philippines to spread Christianity. At the time, the University of Florida graduates and college sweethearts had four children: Christy, age nine; Katie age seven; Robby age four; and Peter age one. During the family's second year in the Philippines, Pam became pregnant with Tim.

The couple had been praying for another son, one who, Bob hoped, would grow up to be an influential preacher and spread Christianity throughout the world. The pregnancy did not go as well as expected, however. Not long after learning she was pregnant, Pam visited a doctor who said she was not carrying a child at all, merely a tumor. He advised her to have it surgically removed as soon as possible. "[He] said it was a mass of fetal tissue and if I didn't get it aborted, then I would die,"[1] Pam says.

She and Bob, however, were convinced she was truly carrying a child, and they decided to continue the pregnancy, even though it was risky. "That's a faith issue,"[2] Pam says. She not only refused the surgery, but she also chose to stop getting medical care for a time, deciding to leave their fate to God.

The pregnancy continued, and Pam's belly continued to grow. She was indeed carrying a fetus, not a tumor. Still, there were many long months ahead, and every day of the pregnancy was filled with worry that the baby would not survive. Pam bled throughout the pregnancy due to a serious complication called a placental abruption. The placenta is a vital organ that connects a fetus to the uterus. It provides the fetus with nutrients and oxygen and removes waste. In a healthy pregnancy, the placenta is firmly attached to the wall of the uterus. However, Pam's placenta had partially detached, a condition that is very dangerous to both the mother and the baby. The fetus is at risk of being deprived of the necessary nutrients and oxygen that allow it to grow and develop normally. The mother, meanwhile, is at constant risk of hemorrhage, or very heavy bleeding. Placental abruption can be deadly, for both the mother and baby.

"Miracle Baby"

Pam's pregnancy became even more complicated when she contracted amoebic dysentery, a serious illness caused by the parasitic protozoan *Entamoeba histolytica*. People usually get it by drinking contaminated water. The microscopic organism infects the large intestine and causes symptoms that include severe abdominal cramping and diarrhea, as well as a high fever. Amoebic dysentery is the third deadliest parasitic infection in the world and kills between forty thousand and one hundred thousand people every year. Uncommon in the United States, amoebic dysentery typically occurs in places with unsanitary living conditions, which leads to contamination of the water supply.

To save Pam's life, doctors prescribed the antibiotic metronidazole. She took one pill before researching the drug and discovering that it could cause birth defects if taken during pregnancy. Although she stopped taking the medication immediately

Pam Tebow is very open about the complications and stress involved in her pregnancy with Tim. She calls him her "miracle baby." Their bond is very strong and evident during football games. Here, mother and son hug following the 2010 Senior Bowl.

and eventually overcame the dysentery without it, the experience added one more worry to a pregnancy that had not gone smoothly from the start.

Complicating the situation even further, the Tebows were living on Mindanao, a poor island in the southern Philippines where health care was lacking. Given the seriousness of Pam's condition and the bleeding in her uterus, she was unable to travel by air to a location that offered better health care. The Tebows had to remain where they were and pray for the best, despite the risk to Pam and the possibility that her baby would die before birth.

Finally, about two months before her due date, Pam's bleeding stopped without explanation. She was able to take a plane to Manila, the capital city of the Philippines, to spend the final weeks of her pregnancy under the care of an American-trained doctor. On August 14, 1987, Pam gave birth to a healthy son, Timothy Richard Tebow, whose first name means "honoring God." "I call him my miracle baby," said Pam in a television commercial that aired during the 2011 Super Bowl. "He almost didn't make it into this world. I remember so many times when I almost lost him. It was so hard."[3]

Despite the pregnancy's many difficulties, Tim started life healthy, if slightly underweight. His family prayed that he would grow up to be strong and fit. By the time the Tebows left the Philippines, Tim was three years old. He had grown so big that his sister, Katie, who had the habit of toting him around, developed two hernias, which the family teasingly blamed on Tim and his large size.

The Family Farm

The Tebows moved back to Florida, and not long after, they bought a 44-acre (18ha) farm just outside the city of Jacksonville. Tim grew up there among cows, horses, chickens, and other animals.

The farm had plenty of room for Tim to follow his two older brothers into all of their games and adventures. "It was a great place to have five kids grow up and work," Tebow says. "I think

 Lanham Christian School
8400 Good Luck Rd.
Lanham, MD 20706

that built as much character in us as anything else."[4] The farm, the physically difficult chores, and the Tebow boys' intensely competitive spirit all planted roots for Tim's signature work ethic to excel at the sports he grew to love best—baseball, basketball, and, especially, football.

Homeschooled

As a child, Tim's days were a blend of farm chores, Bible study, out-door sports with his brothers, and school lessons with his mother. Just as she did with her older children, Pam homeschooled Tim from kindergarten through twelfth grade. Pam specially tailored lessons to each of her children's talents and needs. For Tim's sister, Christy, for example, the focus was on Christy's passion for music and on playing the piano. For Tim and his brother, Robby, the personalized school program allowed them to work in ways that

Tim and brother Robby both suffer from dyslexia, and benefited from their mother's individualized homeschool approach to learning.

helped compensate for their dyslexia, a learning disability that affects a person's ability to make sense of written symbols.

Dyslexia is a genetic condition, which means a person who has it also has a parent who has it. Tim's father, Bob, is also dyslexic. The learning disability makes it hard to learn to read and write, but Pam did not allow her sons to use dyslexia as an excuse to get out of schoolwork or do poorly on lessons. Instead, she crafted her sons' lessons to capitalize on their strengths and let them learn at their own pace. They often learned by doing projects in addition to merely reading about a topic. This helped them make connections between what they were reading and what it meant.

In addition to typical school subjects, the Tebow children also studied the Bible as part of each school day. Every week they were responsible for memorizing and reciting a new batch of biblical quotes and passages. As a result, all five Tebow children developed the ability to quote the Bible at length. Like all of their siblings, Tim and Robby eventually went on to receive college scholarships and obtain college degrees.

When they were not studying or doing chores, Tim and his brothers often played sports, especially baseball, basketball, and football. Even though Tim was the youngest, his siblings took no pity on him and expected him to play (and in the case of football, to get tackled) just as hard as they did. "I had two brothers who beat me at everything, at every turn, as badly as they could," Tebow writes in his book, *Though My Eyes*. "They took no prisoners. There was no 'letting someone win' because he was younger."[5] For countless hours of their childhood, the boys pitched baseballs, shot hoops, and tossed a football back and forth on the farm. All three boys went on to play organized youth sports.

Taking to the Field

When Tim first participated in organized sports, Little League T-ball at age five, it was immediately clear that he was fiercely competitive. He disliked hitting the baseball off the tee and insisted that it be pitched to him underhand instead. By the end of the season, he had scored the second-most home runs

Tebow's Other Sport

During his senior year of high school, Tim Tebow faced a huge decision: selecting which university to attend. He also had to decide whether or not to continue playing football. He was equally good at baseball, and professional baseball teams were interested in him.

Unlike professional football, in which players first play with a college team before they join a professional team, professional baseball teams often accept talented athletes right out of high school. Tebow's father encouraged him to consider baseball as an option. Baseball players are paid well, and they tend to have longer athletic careers and a much smaller risk of serious injury than football players. In the end, Tebow chose football, but his baseball skills remain impressive. In 2010, after a private workout at a high school in Memphis, Tennessee, Tebow took a few swings with the school's baseball team and hit twelve of fifteen pitches out of the park.

in the league; the only boy who scored more was two years older than Tim.

Baseball was Tim's first love in sports, and it was also the sport in which he first came to terms with what it meant to win and to lose. "When I hear parents tell their kids today, 'It doesn't matter if you win or lose, as long as you have fun,' I'm puzzled," he writes in *Through My Eyes*. "That's just not how I'm wired. . . . If there's a score, then there's a purpose to the game, beyond having fun—it's having a greater score."[6] In one of his early baseball games, he chased down a runner for an out instead of throwing the ball to the catcher because Tim thought the catcher was likely to drop the ball and let the opponent score. Tim simply hated to lose.

This early obsession with sports and winning spurred Tim to play and practice during every spare moment. When he was only five years old, he began to build a physical presence that

Tebow's love of sports and desire to be the best on the field started when he was just five years old playing Little League baseball.

would never let him down in competition. His parents attached a length of surgical rubber tubing to the top of a door frame in his house, and he used it constantly, working his arms and shoulders by pulling down repeatedly against the tubing's resistance. He wanted to build stronger arm muscles to pitch baseballs in Little League and make difficult shots in his church basketball league. He also dreamed of excelling at football, a sport that he eventually discovered he wanted to play most of all.

Becoming a Quarterback

During the summer that he turned eight years old, Tim joined Pop Warner, a youth football organization, and began his first football season with the Lakeshore Athletic Association near Jacksonville. He was big, strong, fast, and aggressive, and he made a name for himself on the field. "Everybody in the Jacksonville Pop Warner community seems to have a tale about Tebow," writes reporter Dave Curtis in a December 2007 article for the *Orlando Sentinel* newspaper. "They remember Tebow scoring touchdowns. They remember Tebow running over and through players, sometimes knocking them out of games." Tim was, Curtis writes, "smarter, stronger and better than his football-playing peers."[7]

Those early Pop Warner games did much to prepare Tim for a promising future in the sport. He ran, dodged, tackled, and learned to thrive in a very physically demanding game. Tim's size, competitiveness, and fearlessness marked him as an ideal offensive football player. At first he played tight end, a player whose role is often to block the other team's defensive players during offensive plays but also to catch passes. His bulk and strength made him a good fit for the position, but when Tim was eleven years old, his Pop Warner coach, David Hess, had different plans for him. "Guess that's my claim to fame," says Hess. "I'm the one who put him at quarterback."[8] The move changed Tim's outlook on football. He would never again be satisfied playing any other position.

The Shaping of an Athlete

In his early teens, while he was still playing Pop Warner football, Tim received a weight set as a Christmas gift. For years he had begged his parents for one and was excited to start a lifting program. However, Tim's father, who had majored in health and human performance in college, was concerned about the stress an overly aggressive weight-lifting program might put on a still-developing body. He put strict limits on the amount of weight Tim was allowed to lift. Nevertheless, Tim began a rigorous weight regimen, which he added to the four hundred push-ups and four hundred sit-ups he was already doing every day. He also studied books on fitness and bodybuilding and crafted a fitness program for himself that borrowed elements from the regimen his eldest brother, Robby, was using as a college football player. Tim also threw in some techniques he learned from his best friend's father, who was a U.S. Navy SEAL, a member of the Navy's elite special forces unit whose members undergo physically rigorous sea, air, and land (SEAL) training and complete some of the most dangerous operations required by the U.S. military.

By the time he started eighth grade, Tim had gained muscle bulk from his bodybuilding. Muscle tissue is heavy, and he now weighed too much to continue playing in the Pop Warner league. He tried out instead for the junior varsity team at Jacksonville's Trinity Christian Academy, a private high school where Tim's brothers had played football. Although younger than his teammates, Tim not only made the junior varsity team, but he also played quarterback. In this position he led his team to an undefeated season. When the junior varsity season ended, the varsity team's longer season was still going, and Tim moved to that team to help finish its season.

Tim made the school's varsity team again the following year, playing as a freshman. Because he was homeschooled, his parents were able to organize his school lessons around his rigorous physical training regimen, practices, and games. Tim joined the varsity team eager to play at the position he loved best—quarterback. Unfortunately, his unwavering commitment to bodybuilding worked against him. He was larger, stronger, and more athletic than many of his teammates, and quarterbacks usually do not run as much or get as physical as players in other field positions, such as linebacker and running back. The team's coach thought the hulking freshman was too athletic to play quarterback and that his size, speed, and strength could be put to better use in other positions.

As a result, Tim spent his freshman football season at Trinity playing linebacker and running back. He also played basketball and baseball for the school, but he never lost sight of his goal of being quarterback. Being assigned other positions for being too athletic frustrated him. "Playing quarterback is what Timmy wanted to do," remembers Bob. "He had a dream, a passion to do that. Other coaches wanted him to play linebacker like his brothers, who were good linebackers. When I looked at Timmy, he didn't have that magic at linebacker. When you put him on the other side of the ball, he had a lot of magic."[9] Even though his family had a long athletic history with Trinity Christian Academy,

Tim decided to leave the school's football team after his freshman year in search of a high school program that would allow him to pursue his dream of playing quarterback.

A New Venue

Being homeschooled had not interfered with Tim's ability to play sports at Trinity—but it was a private school that did not take money from the state government. It therefore was not obligated to follow the same regulations that the state's tax-funded public schools had to follow with regard to participants in sports. When Tim started looking for other high schools to play for as a sophomore, he realized that being homeschooled could put him at a disadvantage. Laws in Florida allow students who are homeschooled to participate in sports at public schools but only

Tebow aspired to play high school football for Craig Howard (left). When Tebow was honored with the Heisman Trophy, Howard and college coach Urban Meyer (right) posed for photos.

if they live in the same county as the school where they play. Tim was selective. He did not want to play for just any high school or just any coach. He set his heart on playing for Craig Howard, whose offensive coaching style centered around a quarterback who could throw the ball.

Howard was coach at Nease High School in Saint Johns County. The Tebows did not live in Saint Johns County, so Tim and his mother rented an apartment close to the school so Tim could qualify for play. This did not really affect the rest of the family because, by this time, all of Tim's siblings were either at college or living on their own, and his father spent a lot of time traveling for his missionary work in the Philippines. Tim finished his high school years living primarily with his mom, doing schoolwork in their apartment, and playing football.

Championships

Tim's sophomore football season at Nease was neither magnificent nor terrible, although he suffered hardship. In the middle of the season, during the first half of the game against rival Saint Augustine High School, Tim broke his fibula, the smaller of the two bones in the lower leg. He went to the sidelines, where Howard told him it was probably just a bruise. Howard recalls, "I felt like a bad coach later. He played the rest of the game and scored on a 29-yard touchdown run on a broken leg to tie the game in the fourth quarter." A visit to the hospital later revealed the true extent of the injury. "The X-ray showed a jagged break of his lower leg," Howard says. "That showed me how tough he was."[10]

The broken leg put an end to Tim's sophomore year of play midseason, and the team finished the season with five wins and five losses. Tim believed they could do much better. The following season, when he returned for his junior year as quarterback, he led the team to a much-improved season with eleven wins and two losses. Both defeats were to archrival Saint Augustine—one during the regular season, the other during the second round of playoffs for the state championship.

The Chosen One

Faces of Sports: Tim Tebow, The Chosen One is a one-hour documentary about Tim Tebow created by ESPN, a sports entertainment company that includes television cable networks, radio stations, websites, and magazines. First aired on the ESPN cable network in December 2005, the film features footage of Tebow leading his Nease High School team to victory, his experiences as a homeschooler, and his college selection process.

ESPN subtitled the documentary *The Chosen One*, a term with religious overtones that refers to a hero who, as if by destiny, has superhuman abilities or character and a special mission. In choosing this title, ESPN may have helped set off the publicity frenzy that has followed Tebow. Many people believe he is indeed a chosen one. Others, however, scoff at the hype and find the title one more reason to criticize the quarterback. Tebow himself has never referred to himself this way and claimed to be somewhat embarrassed by the title of the documentary. The nickname stuck with him anyway, raising people's expectations to nearly impossible heights and drawing sharp criticism if Tebow fails to meet them.

Despite the two losses that kept Nease from a state title, Tim's playing style drew attention. "He amazed me the first time I saw him," says Howard. "He continues to amaze me. . . . I knew he was going to do some special things."[11] Tim's fellow players, too, looked on as the community began to take note of a rising star. "Even other players came up to him," says Ryan Ellis, one of Tim's fellow players at Nease. "They'd get out of their jerseys and ask about autographs. Back then, it was a little hard getting used to. We [had] never encountered a man like Timmy."[12]

In the fall of 2005, going into his senior year of play, Tim was leading a team everyone knew could be a challenger for the division 4A state title in Florida. He had already garnered attention

In 2005 Tebow (second to left) joined Josh Freeman, Pat Devlin, Neil Caudle, Jevan Snead, and Matthew Stafford as part of the EA Elite 11 Quarterback Camp at SOKA University in Aliso Viejo, California.

from coaches of some of the nation's best college teams. In the face of all the hype, he did not disappoint his rapidly growing fan base. Nease capped its season by making it to the Florida 4A championship game against Armwood High School. During the game, Tim passed for more than 200 yards (183m) and four touchdowns and rushed for more than 150 yards (137m), scoring another two touchdowns. Nease won the state championship with a final score of 44–37.

Tim was the undisputed star of the championship game, having contributed to every point Nease scored. The 6-foot-3, 225-pound (102kg) teenager was named 2005 Mr. Florida Football and was featured that year in a documentary titled *The Chosen One*. Football fans everywhere wondered which college he would play for the following year.

Chapter 2

Into the Gator Swamp

Even after leading his high school football team to a state championship and twice being named Florida's high school football player of the year, Tim Tebow was just one of thousands of talented high school athletes nationwide vying for football scholarships at prestigious universities—especially the ones that were potential contenders for national college titles. Only the best athletes stand out, especially for the top-tier teams on which Tebow had set his sights. Furthermore, university recruiters (university representatives who decide which players they would like to add to their school's team) look at more than just athletic achievement; the fact that Tebow had been homeschooled put him in a potentially risky academic situation. Although Tebow had the character and intelligence to succeed in football and school, his atypical schooling experience was a potential barrier to college, both academically and athletically.

Proving Himself to Recruiters

University recruiters had watched Tebow throughout his high school football career at Nease. After his senior season, he was one of just seventy-eight high school players from around the country chosen for *Parade* magazine's 2005 All America Football Team, an annual list of the nation's best-performing high school football players. Recruiters focus on the players on this list,

After receiving a great amount of recruiting attention, including scholarship offers from eighty colleges, Tebow made his decision to attend the University of Florida.

and they considered Tebow a very desirable prospect. While his football skills were well-known, however, he faced a possible disadvantage in one area all recruiters ask about: academic performance.

Being homeschooled since kindergarten meant Tebow did not have a grade point average (GPA) that recruiters could use to compare him academically with other players. "As important as talent is on the football field, earning the grades good enough to be able to get into a university and stay eligible [to play football is] just as important," says sports journalist and former college football player Clarence K. Moniba. There are college sports rules that say if an athlete gets poor grades, then he or she becomes ineligible, which means that he or she is not allowed to compete. "Coaches want to see in players the ability to excel in their schoolwork as a reassurance that they won't be dealing with ineligibility problems throughout their college career,"[13] says Moniba. The absence of a standard high school transcript and a school guidance counselor who could attest to Tebow's academic competence had the possibility of setting him back in the recruitment process.

Tebow, however, was undaunted. As a high school freshman, he had taken the Scholastic Aptitude Test (SAT), a standardized test required for college admission. Despite his dyslexia, he received a score of 890—high enough to qualify him for college admission even before he had completed most of his high school coursework. He claimed a high school grade point average of 3.5 in his homeschool curriculum as well, which translates to an average of As and Bs. It positioned him competitively among other recruits.

Finding no academic reason to eliminate the homeschooler from consideration, recruiters from all over the country wanted the quarterback. Tebow received scholarship offers from eighty schools. "In this day and age of the spread offense at the college level, Tebow's talents are the perfect recipe for success," said Tom Luginbill, national college recruiting director for Scouts Inc. "With so much emphasis being placed on the quarterback's ability to run and throw, guys like him are becoming a hot commodity."[14]

A Tough Decision

For Tebow, the difficult part about the recruitment process was choosing from dozens of good offers. "It's one of the toughest decisions I'll ever have to make," he told news reporters. "There's a lot of good programs, but you have to be wise about it."[15] He

Statuesque

As a result of his record-breaking performance as a Florida Gator, Tim Tebow's name will forever be etched in University of Florida memory. In April 2011 the campus unveiled another way to remember the famed quarterback: a life-size statue of him outside the university's football field. The

Tebow left behind a huge legacy at his alma mater. On April 9, 2011, life-sized statues of Tim Tebow, Danny Wuerffel, and Steve Spurrier (Florida Heisman trophy winners) were unveiled outside of

approximately 2,000-pound (907kg) bronze statue joined the statues of Steve Spurrier and Danny Wuerffel, Florida's two other Heisman Trophy winners. Spurrier's and Wuerffel's likenesses rear back their arms in a football-passing pose. Tebow's has the ball tucked beneath its arm as if preparing to run for a score.

The bronze figure is not the first time Tebow has been memorialized in statuary. While he was still a student at Florida, a chainsaw artist carved his 8-foot likeness into a dead tree outside Ballyhoo Grill, a popular restaurant. When the NCAA heard of the statue, it told the University of Florida to have the restaurant remove or change it. According to NCAA rules, current college athletes' likenesses cannot be used to promote any businesses or products. The Ballyhoo Grill complied by changing the number on the statue's jersey to seven, Wuerffel's former number, but after Tebow graduated from college, his jersey number fifteen was repainted. The carving has always affectionately been known as Treebow.

spent his free time in the fall of his senior year traveling to university campuses and meeting coaches. He finally narrowed his choices to two schools—the University of Alabama and his home state's University of Florida. On December 13, 2005, he made it official: He would play football for Florida, the school his parents had attended and whose orange and blue colors had decorated his bedroom since childhood.

Having worked hard on his studies, Tebow was ready to graduate a semester early so he could enroll as a student at Florida and be there for spring football training during what would be other recruits' final semester of high school. The day before the start of the spring semester, Tebow was cleared to enroll in college classes as an official student. He packed his things, moved to an apartment near campus, and became a Gator, the University of Florida's mascot and the name its students call themselves. He arrived just in time for the strenuous spring training.

Working Harder than Anyone Else

Since the Gators already had an outstanding senior quarterback, Chris Leak, lined up for the following year, Tebow was not a starting player for his first college season, meaning he was not in the best group of players who are sent onto the field first during every game unless they are injured or cannot play for some reason. However, Tebow was no average freshman, either. During the spring's physical conditioning drills, his coaches and teammates quickly developed respect for his strength, determination, and attitude. "He's ready to go," Florida coach Urban Meyer said during the spring training season. "Tim Tebow is ready to go play quarterback at Florida."[16] The coaches knew they had a powerful backup quarterback on the sidelines who could be a secret weapon.

In the first game of 2006 against the University of Southern Mississippi, Tebow was called to play in the game during the fourth quarter. Wearing jersey number fifteen, Tebow ran down the field with the ball and scored his first college touchdown.

Tebow leaves Ben Hill Griffin Stadium, victorious after defeating the Southern Mississippi Golden Eagles 34–7. Tebow scored his first college touchdown in the fourth quarter of the game.

He was a freshman player inexperienced in the Southeastern Conference (SEC), one of the most competitive college football conferences (groups of university and college teams that compete against each other) in the National Collegiate Athletic Association (NCAA), but Florida's coaches wanted to find out what Tebow could do. In the season's second game, they put him in to play several times in the second half. By the third game, against the University of Tennessee, the coaches had created a few special plays just for Tebow. In the fourth game, against the University of Kentucky, at the Gators' home stadium, Tebow threw the first touchdown pass of his college career. By then, Florida fans were clamoring to see more of number fifteen.

Tebow, still the second-string quarterback, was scoring points both rushing (carrying the ball down the field) and passing (throwing the ball to a teammate). In the season's sixth game, against Louisiana State University (LSU), he thrilled fans by completing a jump pass, running with the ball and then jumping to throw it over the other team's defense to an open receiver, for a touchdown in the final seconds of the first half. The move was the first in a string of spectacular jump passes and last-moment saves that would become part of Tebow lore. His contributions helped his team on their march to the conference championship versus the University of Arkansas, a game Florida won to clinch the conference title. The Gators would play in the national championship game versus undefeated and number one–ranked Ohio State University in January 2007. Tebow was where he had always wanted to be—on a team vying for a national championship.

Florida was widely considered the underdog in the game against Ohio State, but the Gators' defense was among the best of any college team. It held Ohio State to just two touchdowns. Florida's offense, meanwhile, racked up forty-one points in the game, with Tebow contributing two touchdowns as a second-string quarterback—one by running the ball into the end zone, the other with a pass. "Florida freshman Tim Tebow continued to impress me with his ability to feel the soft spot of a defense and then do the power running,"[17] wrote ESPN college football analyst Jim Donnan after the game. The Florida Gators won the game and became a national champion. Fans were eager to see how Tebow would follow the 2006–2007 season when he returned as a sophomore as Florida's starting quarterback.

Quarterback Qualities

Tebow's second year at Florida began with uncertainty. Many of the team's seniors had graduated, and he was surrounded by new teammates, which created a different team dynamic than that of the year before. Although still a young player on the team, Tebow wanted to set a good example. He subjected himself to the hardest physical workouts during the spring, attended all his

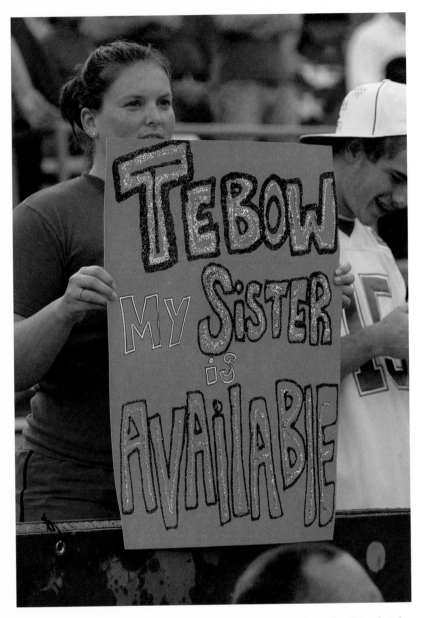

Many fans admire Tebow for his high moral code, his faith, and his charitable work. Aware that he is a public figure, he is careful to preserve a role model image. This Tebow fan holds a sign at a University of Florida game, showing the quarterback her sister is available for a date.

classes, earned straight As, and did not party before games. In the season-opening game against Western Kentucky University in the fall of 2007, Tebow showed he had the skills to be a starting quarterback on a national championship team. He threw for 300 passing yards (274m) during the game, leading Florida to a 49–3 win. "He's going to be a great player here," Coach Meyer said. "He's going to will himself into the end zone many times here."[18]

The Gators kept racking up points, beating Troy University 59–31 and the University of Tennessee 59–20. During the Tennessee game, Tebow scored four touchdowns, two passing and two rushing. He was making a name for himself as a dual threat in college football—a quarterback equally gifted at throwing scoring passes and at charging through lines of defenders to score on foot. His size, strength, determination, and intuition made him a standout on the field. By the third game of his sophomore season, ESPN sportscasters were saying that Tebow could be a candidate for the Heisman Trophy, awarded each year to the most outstanding player in college football. After the season's fourth game, a win against the University of Mississippi, Tebow was named the SEC's offensive player of the week for the second time that season.

The Gators' winning streak came to an end with a narrow loss to Auburn University on Florida's home field. By this time, Tebow's name was well-known around the nation and especially by Florida's main rivals, among them LSU. The week following the Auburn loss, Florida played LSU at LSU's home field. In the days leading up to the game, Tebow was heckled incessantly by LSU fans who had obtained his cell phone number. He received hundreds of offensive and threatening calls and text messages every day that week. In the stands during the game, LSU fans shouted an anti-Tebow chant. Much as Tebow wanted a win in the face of all the heckling, the Gators suffered another narrow defeat, losing to LSU 24–28. The loss knocked them out of the running for the SEC championship and any chance to play for a national title that year. Tebow's stardom, however, was still gaining strength and speed.

Titles and Trophies

Despite losing two important games, Tebow played harder than ever for the rest of his sophomore season. In a game against the University of Kentucky, he sprained and dislocated his right shoulder. Even though he throws with his left hand, the painful injury still affected his performance. Tebow played the rest of the Kentucky game anyway, and every other game during the season, even though he needed a painkiller injected into his shoulder before games and practices. Following the Gators' loss to the University of Georgia the week after his injury, Georgia coach Mark Richt said Tebow's pain and scaled-back performance were noticeable. "We knew he had gotten hurt," Richt said. "As the game went on, it was pretty evident that they were not going to run him as much as normal. I just had to assume that his shoulder was bothering him."[19]

Tebow soldiered on, and two weeks later, despite shoulder pain so severe he could hardly lift his right arm, he led a winning effort against South Carolina, running for five touchdowns and contributing to two others with his rushing and passing skills. Florida won its final two games of the season as well; Tebow playing through to the end, even after breaking his hand when it was smashed between the colliding helmets of two opposing players during the last game of the 2007 season against the Gators' archrival, Florida State. "He deserves to be mentioned again for the Heisman," Florida State coach Bobby Bowden said. "I don't know if I've ever seen a better leader."[20]

Despite his efforts, Tebow did not lead his team back to the national championships his first year as starting quarterback. But he did lead the way to big awards. He was named the Walter Camp All-American, an award named after a pioneer of American football and recognizing the nation's best college football player, as chosen by a committee. He earned the AAU (Amateur Athletic Union) Sullivan Award for being the nation's best amateur athlete (the first time the award had gone to a football player in a decade). He won the Maxwell Award for the College Player of the Year and the Davey O'Brien National Quarterback Award. And on December 9, 2007, Tebow took

University of Florida quarterback Tim Tebow was a highly-decorated athlete in 2007, winning prestigous awards such as the Maxwell Award, the Walter Camp All-American Award, and the Heisman Trophy. He was the first sophomore to be granted the Heisman.

home the biggest and most coveted award in all of college sports, the Heisman Trophy, becoming the first sophomore to win it since the award's creation in 1935.

Playing in Verse

Winning a Heisman with two college years left to play only made Tebow more determined. At the start of his junior year, he had his eyes not on more trophies but on the SEC and national titles that had eluded Florida the year before. He increased his efforts in strength and endurance workouts, as did his teammates, and they started the 2008 fall season with a 56–10 win against the University of Hawaii on Hawaii's home field.

By the season's second game, Tebow and the Gators had settled on a new goal: to become the only team in University of Florida history to complete an undefeated football season. Even with his shoulder injury still nagging him, Tebow helped lead his team to a 26–3 win over the University of Miami and a 30–6 win over the University of Tennessee. He also began a tradition that would follow him for the rest of his college days; he picked up a white permanent marker and wrote a Bible verse onto his eye-black stickers, the dark patches athletes wear under their eyes during games to help reduce glare. Tebow wrote "PHIL" beneath his right eye and "4:13" beneath his left. Phil. 4:13 is the abbreviation for Bible verse Philippians 4:13, which states, "I can do all things through Him who strengthens me."[21] Tebow wore the eye-black inscription during games for the rest of the season.

The Promise

Unfortunately, the Bible verse was not a self-fulfilling prophecy. The Gators lost their fourth game by one point to the University of Mississippi, dashing their hopes for an undefeated season. Crushed by the loss to a team he thought the Gators should have beaten, Tebow appeared in a press conference after the game and delivered the following speech:

I just want to say one thing. To the fans and everybody in Gator Nation [University of Florida fans], I'm sorry, extremely sorry. I promise you one thing, a lot of good will come out of this. You will never see any player in the entire country play as hard as I will play the rest of the season, and you will never see someone push the rest of the team as hard as I will push everybody the rest of the season, and you will never see a team play harder than we will the rest of the season. God bless.[22]

ESPN and other sports networks aired Tebow's speech, which became one of the most notable speeches ever made by a college athlete. Tebow and the rest of his team made good on what became known as simply "The Promise." They won every game

Adding a Bible verse to his eye black became a Tebow tradition during his collegiate career.

A Record Setter

In 2010 the Bleacher Report website named Tim Tebow one of the ten best college football players of all time. "Tebow emerged as one of the greatest college players to ever step on a football field in his time at Florida, and it began right from the start," writes sportswriter Michael Pinto. As a sophomore, Tebow captured every major national award in college football, becoming the first sophomore ever to win the Heisman Trophy and to earn All-American honors. He was the first football player in NCAA history to rush for twenty touchdowns and also pass for twenty touchdowns in a single season. He was the first college player to be a finalist for three Heisman Trophies. He set a Southeastern Conference (SEC) record for total offense during his college career, passing and rushing for 12,232 yards and 145 touchdowns. That 145-touchdown total also put him in second place in the NCAA Football Bowl Division record charts. When Tebow went to his first NFL play-off game in 2012, he still held Florida high school records, too, for total offense, career passing yards, touchdowns, and completed passes.

Michael Pinto. "The 50 Greatest College Football Players of All Time." Bleacher Report, November 29, 2010. http://bleacherreport.com/articles/528267-the-top-50-college-football-players-of-all-time#/articles/528267-the-top-50-college-football-players-of-all-time/page/43.

the rest of the 2008 season, beating the University of Alabama to secure the SEC championship.

Having won their conference title, Florida went on to play the number-one-ranked University of Oklahoma for the Bowl Championship Series (BCS) national championship. Oklahoma was a formidable opponent, having scored more points in one season than any other team in college football history. In preparation for the game, Tebow made a small but significant change to his appearance; he changed the Bible verse beneath his eyes to "John 3:16." That verse reads, "For God so loved the world, that He gave His only begotten Son, that whoever believes in Him shall not perish, but have eternal life."[23] He had decided earlier in the season to make the change if his team played for a national championship. Whatever happened on the field that night—whether the Gators survived the game to come out winners or saw their championship dreams perish—the Bible verse would remind Tebow that there was more to his life and faith than the outcome of one game.

Tebow and his teammates went on to beat Oklahoma 24–14, winning the Gators' second national football title in Tebow's college career and keeping the promise he had made to his fans. "I felt like he was a prophet for saying it [The Promise]," says Brandon Spikes, who was a linebacker for Florida that year. "He just said it and we got it done."[24]

Stunning Senior

Tebow was nominated for a second Heisman Trophy in 2008, after leading his team to a national title his junior year. He did not win, but he decided to stay at Florida for his senior year instead of leaving college early to enter the National Football League (NFL) draft, the process through which professional football teams pick their players. In the spring of 2009 he had surgery to repair his injured shoulder, and the following fall he led Florida to win its first three games. At that point the team had played thirteen consecutive games without a loss, including the final ten games of the 2008 season. It had the longest winning streak of any college team in the nation.

That streak was tested when Tebow and several of his teammates came down with the H1N1 virus, commonly known as swine flu. They were sick for almost a week and had to miss practices, but Tebow still managed to join the team for its fourth game against the University of Kentucky. He was determined to play, even though he was still dehydrated from his illness and needed to receive fluids intravenously on the sidelines.

Tebow leaves the Kentucky game by ambulance after suffering a head injury. Medical results would prove the superstar quarterback had a concussion.

Then Tebow suffered something far more serious than the flu. As he prepared to throw the ball to a teammate after taking the snap, a Kentucky player charged him and knocked him backward. Tebow's helmet collided with the knee of one of his own players. He lost consciousness and was carried off the field and taken to a hospital by ambulance. Doctors feared the hit had damaged his spinal cord. Although tests showed Tebow's neck and spine were not hurt, he had suffered a severe concussion, an injury in which the head is struck so hard that the brain slams against the inside of the skull. Concussions can cause brain damage. They are especially risky to football players who do not take enough time to heal, because another head injury too soon after receiving one can be deadly. Doctors told Tebow to spend several days in his apartment with no lights, television, music, or reading. The team had two weeks off between games, and Tebow used the time to recover enough to play against Louisiana State University.

Despite Tebow's insistence that he felt fine, the coaches were worried that he would play too hard too soon. He therefore spent most of the game passing the ball instead of running for touchdowns. Even with Tebow at less than full strength, Florida beat LSU, but only by one touchdown. "So much of our offense was predicated upon the possibility that I would rush the ball, but everyone knew—especially LSU's defense—that wasn't going to happen," Tebow writes in *Through My Eyes*. "At the end of the day, that was a good win against a very good team."[25] Several games later, fully healed and back to his characteristic rushing pattern, Tebow broke the SEC record for all-time rushing touchdowns in a college career. Florida won every game in its 2009 regular season, finally earning the undefeated status Tebow had sought since his first day on the field.

Finishing Strong

The Gators played the 2009 SEC championship game against Alabama, and they lost for the first and only time during Tebow's senior year. The defeat kept them from playing for another national title, but Tebow was nominated for the Heisman Trophy again that year. Although he did not win it, he became the first three-time Heisman nominee in history. Florida then played in the Sugar Bowl football game against the University of Cincinnati, where Tebow capped his college football career by carrying or throwing the football for 533 yards (487m) of total offense, the most yardage amassed by a single player in a single bowl game in the history of the BCS.

Tebow graduated from the University of Florida with honors, carrying a 3.66 grade point average and earning a bachelor's degree in family, youth, and community sciences. He was also the most-decorated and award-winning player in national college football history. A plaque inscribed with the words of his 2008 Promise speech is posted outside the university's football complex, and Tebow became a member of the University of Florida Hall of Fame. Having forged a lasting legacy, Tebow bid farewell to Florida and looked forward to the NFL draft in 2010.

Chapter 3

Going Pro

After completing one of the most successful quarterback careers in the history of college football, Tebow faced recruiters again, this time for the NFL draft. Similar to college recruitment, in which universities seek good players so their team is better equipped to win championships, professional football teams also pursue great players to put together the best team possible to win games, but they also choose players for the purpose of trading them for players who are already on other teams in order to get players they want. Professional football teams, or franchises, are huge businesses in the United States, and millions of fans follow the NFL draft closely each year, with experts, commentators, and pundits publicly scrutinizing every team's selections and every athlete. In the spring of 2010 Tebow was often in the news as everyone debated whether the college phenomenon would succeed at the professional level.

Prepping for the Draft

Tebow, along with about 250 other college football players, received an invitation to the 2010 NFL scouting combine. This weeklong event takes place every February in Indianapolis, Indiana, where athletes who want to play professional football can showcase their skills. NFL hopefuls compete for the best times or marks in displays of strength, speed, agility, and game skills. All athletes run timed sprints, bench press 225 pounds (102kg) as many times as they can, and jump for height and distance. Officials take their physical measurements and assess their

Tebow entered the 2010 NFL draft alongside much media attention and speculation. He was the twenty-fifth pick, drafted by the Denver Broncos in the first round.

history of injury. The players take a written test to assess their intelligence and decision-making ability. Statistics are recorded for each athlete on a variety of identical measures. Players also perform drills and tests specific to the football position they hope to play, and coaches and team managers interview players who interest them.

Tebow emerged as a top performer at the 2010 combine. He outdid all other quarterbacks at the 20-yard (18m) shuttle run and the three-cone drill that tests the ability to change direction and remain balanced while running at full speed. He also bested his competition at the vertical jump, leaping 38.5 inches (97.8cm) to tie the record for best vertical jump of any quarterback in the history of the combine. Overall Tebow ranked third out of eighty-nine quarterbacks on the basis of his combine performance and college career.

An Unusual Throwing Style

As impressive as Tebow's combine statistics and college history were, recruiters had mixed feelings about his ability to play in the NFL. One thing critics noted was his unusual style of throwing the football. He threw it much like he threw a baseball: He pitched it. Instead of pointing his hand upward to prepare for a throw, he usually held his hand flat and moved into the throw from the side instead of front to back over his shoulder. He also had a habit of winding up for throws with his whole body, holding the ball at or below chest level and often squatting before releasing it. His unusual positioning of the ball meant a longer release time; it took him an average of 0.6 seconds to release the ball for a pass, compared with the 0.4 seconds most NFL quarterbacks average. At the professional level, split seconds count, and a longer release time gives the other team's defense more time to tackle the quarterback before he can throw the ball.

More often than not, Tebow's imperfect throws still reached his intended targets on the football field, and his passing ability was good enough to win a record-breaking number of games in college. In the critical eyes of coaches, sportswriters, and other NFL professionals, however, Tebow's lack of passing finesse and his tendency to run over defenders for rushing yards instead of opting to pass were potential drawbacks, since an NFL quarterback who runs instead of passing accurately risks being tackled and losing the ball. People worried Tebow would be an inconsistent, unreliable passer on an NFL team. "Tim Tebow can't play quarterback in the NFL. I'm convinced of it,"[26] said Todd McShay, ESPN's director of college scouting and one of the most outspoken critics of Tebow during the 2010 NFL draft.

Tebow's pro day, an event that a university sponsors to allow its student athletes to showcase their skills for recruiters from professional teams, gave him an opportunity to show about a hundred NFL coaches, executives, and recruiters a new throwing style he had been practicing. Tebow now held the ball closer to his ear before launching it, and he threw it with speed and accuracy. He demonstrated to coaches that even if he was not a flawless passer, he had the ability and willingness to work on making his throwing style better fit their expectations for an NFL quarterback. "The people who don't think I can make it, that pushes me even more,"[27] Tebow told reporters.

Many coaches were interested, but the draft itself still lay ahead. No one knew which team would take Tebow or how long it would take him to be drafted. "The hardest player to place in Mock Drafts [predictions of what players will be chosen by what teams] is easily Tim Tebow," said draft expert Keet Bailey. "You can't help but wonder what NFL team owner doesn't want this guy strictly for ticket sales and leadership ability, but how high is too high to draft for such a big risk? . . . It's too hard to say where this guy is going to go."[28]

Draft Day Arrives

On April 22, 2010, millions of football fans gathered around televisions to see which NFL teams would take which new players. The draft process occurs in seven rounds: All thirty-two NFL teams take turns choosing from a pool of about three hundred former college athletes seeking spots in the professional league.

Teams get to choose new players in reverse order of their success the previous season, which means the worst-performing team gets to choose first, while the team that won the Super Bowl chooses last in each round. Teams can also trade places in each round with one another. A team designated to choose eighth in the first round, for example, may want a player it thinks will be chosen by another team first. To get that player, the team may trade its place in other rounds, such as choosing later in the second round for a chance to choose earlier in the first. In this way, a team might improve its chances of getting a player it especially wants.

Regardless of what teams do with their choices, or draft picks, the players all share a common hope—to be chosen as early in the draft as possible, since the sooner they are chosen, the more skilled and desirable they are deemed to be and the higher their salary. At the start of the first round of draft picks, Tebow watched the draft at home on television. Unlike his college recruitment, in which he received many offers from top schools and he got to decide where he would play the following year, Tebow did not get to decide which NFL team he would join. In the weeks leading up to the draft, Tebow's throwing style had received harsh criticism, and he was unsure how early he would be picked. The night of the first draft round, he watched and waited as player after player was drafted. The number of teams left to choose in round one dwindled. As the night went on, it looked like Tebow would have to wait until the second round the following day to find out which team he would be playing for.

Finally, toward the end of the first round, the Denver Broncos chose Tebow. He was the twenty-fifth pick of the draft and the second of fourteen quarterbacks to be drafted that year. Denver had traded its second-, third-, and fourth-round draft places in order to get Tebow.

Many Tebow fans were surprised that the Jacksonville Jaguars, of Tebow's hometown of Jacksonville, Florida, had passed on the chance to draft a local hero. But playing for the Broncos in some ways seemed to be fate. The Broncos team uniforms had the same colors, orange and blue, as the Florida Gators. Jersey number fifteen, which Tebow wore for the Gators, was also available at Denver. Tebow just had to move to Colorado. "You are adding one big-time human being on your football team," said Jon Gruden, a former NFL coach and an NFL analyst for ESPN, reacting to the Broncos' decision to take Tebow. "This guy, Tebow, will not be denied. He will develop into a big-time football player. He will be huge in the Broncos' community."[29]

Mile-High Hype

When Tebow arrived in Denver, Colorado, to start training with his new team, his situation mirrored his experience during his first year as a Florida Gator. The Broncos already had a starting and a second-string quarterback. All indications were that Tebow, a rookie once again, would see very little playing time early on, especially during the first season, but many people were curious to see if he would be as exciting a player in the NFL has he had been in college. During spring practices, fans sometimes collected just to watch Tebow's postpractice sprints. At first game of

Tebow was welcomed by a stadium filled with Gators fans at the season opener against the Jacksonsville Jaquars in September 2010.

Something to Believe In

During his time at the University of Florida, Tim Tebow inscribed several different Bible verses on the adhesive eye-black patches he wore under his eyes during games. The most famous of these was John 3:16, which he sported when Florida won the national championship game on January 8, 2009. Exactly three years

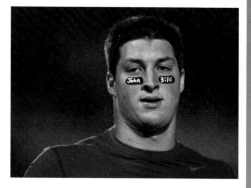

Biblical verse John 3:16 is famously associated to Tebow. Some feel that the number 316 is spiritually connected to him.

later to the day, January 8, 2012, Tebow was playing his first NFL play-off game. Writing on eye black is prohibited in the NFL, but the numbers three, one, and six came up again and again during the game. Tebow passed for exactly 316 yards (289m) and averaged 31.6 yards (28.9m) per completed pass. The Steelers' quarterback threw the game-changing intercepted pass on the third down with 16 yards (15m) to go for another first down, and the Steelers had possession of the ball for exactly thirty-one minutes and six seconds during the game. CBS, the television network that aired the game, reported ratings of 31.6 during the fourth quarter. Doubters scoff at the idea that spiritual influence is behind the religious quarterback's success, but many Tebow fans disagree.

the season in the fall of 2010 against the Jacksonville Jaguars in Florida, Tebow was greeted by a familiar sight—a stadium filled with Florida Gators fans in Tebow jerseys that had turned out mainly to see him.

Tebow had only brief playing time in that first game of his pro career, and the story was the same for the next several games. As the third-string quarterback, he rarely got to play, and even worse, the Broncos rarely took home good news. Toward the end of the 2010 season, the team had one of the worst records in the league and had set a Broncos record for the most losses in a single season and by some of the biggest point deficits the Denver team had seen in years.

By the final three games of the season, the Broncos were beyond all hope of making the playoffs. On December 26, 2010, interim coach Eric Studesville started Tebow at quarterback against the Houston Texans in the third-to-last game of the season. At halftime, the Broncos had yet to score and were down by seventeen points. It looked like another loss was imminent and that Tebow would fulfill widespread predictions that he could not play at the level of the NFL.

Playing Until the End

Tebow was not ready to give up in his first game as a starting NFL quarterback, however. "I am someone who is going to play until the end," he told his teammates at halftime. "I love this game and I am going to play it with all my heart."[30] He then returned to the field and completed several second-half passes that led to touchdowns.

By the start of the fourth quarter, the Broncos had closed the point gap and a win was within reach. With about three minutes left to play, Tebow charged forward and ran for a touchdown that tied the score. The Broncos made the field goal for the extra point and won the game, 24–23. Tebow threw for 308 total passing yards (282m) in that game, more than any Denver quarterback had ever passed in his first game as a starter. Tebow pointed to the sky in his characteristic show of heavenly praise, and the crowd of Denver fans went wild. "He is exactly what you thought coming out of college," Houston coach Gary Kubiak said of Tebow after the game. "He is a winner."[31]

Tebow played in the final two games of the 2010 season with similar flair. Although the Broncos lost both games, Tebow's unorthodox playing style was full of exciting touchdown runs and other surprises. His passes were still far from perfect, and critics found many flaws in the way he played football. Yet the fans did not care. By the end of what had been a depressing season for the Broncos, the stands started filling up with people who just wanted to see Tebow play. Ticket broker SeatGeek reported that high demand drove the cost of tickets to Broncos games up by as much as 44 percent whenever Denver announced that Tebow would be its starting quarterback. Even fans of opposing teams were turning out in greater numbers wherever Tebow was scheduled to take the field.

Second Season Stardom

For the first four weeks of the 2011 season, Tebow again sat on the sidelines, while Denver's coaches started quarterback Kyle Orton. Although the final scores were close, the Broncos lost three of those four games. During every week that Tebow did not play, fans in the crowd chanted his name. In the middle of the fifth game against the San Diego Chargers, Denver's coaches put in Tebow. The Broncos were losing 23–10. By the end of the fourth quarter, Tebow had led the Broncos to within striking range for a win. He released a last attempt at a game-winning pass with just seconds left on the clock. The receiver failed to make the catch and the Broncos lost, but in just two quarters of football, Tebow had changed the dynamics of a game, a team, and a season.

Tebow played starting quarterback for the rest of the games that year, bringing unforgettable, nail-biting moments to the fans. Playing against the Miami Dolphins, for example, the Broncos scored no points until the fourth quarter of the game. Behind 15–0, with just minutes left, Tebow threw one touchdown pass, then another. The Broncos then had thirteen points. Instead of kicking the ball for one extra point after their second touchdown, the Broncos opted for a two-point conversion,

Losing to the New York Jets, Tebow ran 20 yards in the final minute of the November 17, 2011 game. He scored the winning touchdown. He was the first NFL quarterback to achieve such a long touchdown run in the final minute of regulation.

Media Magnet

Everywhere Tim Tebow goes, he leaves a trail of headlines in his wake. The quarterback regularly attracts a far larger crowd of reporters than any other athlete in the vicinity, likely because the public—love him or hate him—is interested in reading and hearing about Tebow. At the NFL scouting combine in February 2010, for example, more than one hundred reporters flocked around Tebow, far more than those who followed any of the three hundred other athletes who turned out to display their skills. Tebow later waited out the tense evening of the NFL draft at home, but even there, the NFL network had camera crews on-site. They were eager to interview him when the Broncos drafted him as a first-round pick.

running a full play to try for two points. They succeeded and tied the game. They went on to win in overtime, becoming the first team in NFL history to be losing by fifteen points with less than three minutes left in the game and to emerge with a victory. "Tebow did some spectacular things there in the last few minutes and got us the win,"[32] said Broncos cornerback Champ Bailey.

Two games later, after a loss to the Detroit Lions, Tebow led the Broncos to a win against the Oakland Raiders and within range of a three-way tie for first place in their NFL division, the AFC (American Football Conference) West. Tebow rushed for 117 yards (107m) during the game, again proving himself a dual threat as an NFL quarterback—one who can both throw the ball and run with it. "Tebow's got the ball in his hands and he's dangerous,"[33] said Broncos running back Willis McGahee after the game. With Tebow as quarterback, the Broncos turned what had been another losing season into a chance at a division title with two more fourth-quarter Tebow comebacks. Against the New York Jets, Tebow ran for a 20-yard (18m), winning touchdown in the final minute. No other quarterback in NFL history had ever run such a long, winning touchdown sprint with just sixty seconds left in a game.

"He Did It Again and Again"

The Broncos made it to the play-offs, and Tebow was still not done working late-game miracles. Against the Pittsburgh Steelers in a game that went into overtime, Tebow completed an 80-yard (73m) touchdown pass in just eleven seconds against the Steelers' star defense, helping the Broncos win one of the most memorable play-off games in recent NFL history. "The heavily favored Steelers were upset by the Broncos because they underestimated Tim Tebow," writes ESPN sports reporter and commentator Jamison Hensley. "Pittsburgh dared the struggling quarterback to beat the NFL's top-ranked defense by throwing deep, and he did it again and again."[34]

Although the Broncos went on to the division title game and lost, Tebow gained notoriety with his last-minute game-saving maneuvers. He earned praise for his solid work ethic and commitment to the game. "Tim works as hard as any player I've ever coached," says John Fox, head coach of the Broncos. "He goes out to practice early, stays late and comes in on his day off. Tim does everything in his power to get better."[35]

Although his fourth-quarter and overtime saves endeared him to millions of cheering fans, they also gave his critics fodder. In the 2011 season Tebow completed relatively few good passes in the first three quarters of a given game, but his number of completed passing yards tended to triple during the fourth quarter. Critics used this as proof that three-fourths of the time, Tebow played poorly. Legions of Tebow admirers, however, saw the quarterback's string of strong fourth quarters as proof of his unwavering faith in himself, his team, and God.

Tebow finished his second pro season to mixed reviews. Some saw his playing style as both inspired and inspirational. Others saw it as desperate. In October 2011 the Bleacher Report website named him the fourteenth most divisive athlete of all time for gathering devoted fans and harsh critics in almost equal measure. By mixing open demonstrations of faith with not-always-flawless football, Tebow had become a highly controversial sports figure.

Chapter 4

A Controversial Career

Tim Tebow has one of the nation's most famous names and faces. Shortly after leading the Broncos' upset play-off win against the Steelers, an ESPN sports poll named him the most popular athlete in America. *Time* magazine ranked Tebow in its list of the one hundred most influential people of 2012. His name has headlined countless newspaper stories and was plastered on Colorado billboards imploring Broncos coaches to "play Tebow." Although he was a starting quarterback for only half the 2011 season, Tebow's number fifteen Denver Broncos jersey led those of all other NFL players in sales. Tebow's autobiography, *Through My Eyes*, debuted at number six on the *New York Times* nonfiction best-seller list in June 2011. He has developed a fan base that numbers in the millions.

For every "I Support Tim Tebow" or "Tim Tebow Believers" Facebook page that exists, however, there is one for Tebow detractors. The quarterback's larger-than-life reputation comes as much from what some Americans find annoying about him as from what others seem to adore. Much of the debate about his likeability stems from his unorthodox style of playing football, which stirs love-hate conflicts among fans, and he is divisive not just athletically but also religiously and politically.

The Tebow Paradox

Tebow seems to become a hometown hero anywhere he plays football, even though most analysts of the sport say he is far from the best NFL quarterback in the nation. Part of the paradox is that sometimes Tebow plays poorly. He has the build of a player who tackles, not one who primarily throws. He plows fearlessly into lines of defenders, an activity most NFL coaches discourage in their quarterbacks because it often leads to injury. Quarterbacks are instead prized for their ability to call the plays and lead the team's offense. Tebow passes less often than most other quarterbacks do, frequently throws incomplete passes, and sometimes plays by instinct rather than following his team's drawn-up play. Top-rated NFL quarterbacks, such as Tom Brady of the New England Patriots and Aaron Rodgers of the Green Bay Packers, complete a higher percentage of their passes and have a much more predictable playing style than Tebow does. Still, Tebow eclipses most other quarterbacks in popularity, confounding critics. "He prays and wins—and America abides, jaws agape, ready to devour every bit of him we can,"[36] writes sportswriter Ryan Klocke.

What Tebow brings to every game, and what may be responsible for his popularity, is suspense. Occasional flubs aside, he has moments of sheer greatness that take everyone by surprise and often lead to winning scores. Nobody watching Tebow or playing against him ever knows exactly what he will do. People have watched him perform football miracles, turning seemingly insurmountable point deficits into wins in the final moments of a game or throwing nearly impossible passes perfectly when it matters most. Tebow seems to play his best when the pressure is highest, and as long as he is in striking distance, no opponent feels safe until the clock has run out. He brings thrills and excitement to football, and his presence on the field both packs the stands and keeps them full until the game is over. If Tebow makes one of his famous last-minute plays to pull off an underdog win, no one wants to miss it. "Love him or hate him, you have to watch him,"[37] says ESPN contributor Amanda Rykoff.

Hearts for Tebow

Tim Tebow is considered one of the country's most eligible bachelors. Women in the stands of his games hold up handmade signs proposing marriage. There were rumors that he may have dated Olympic skier Lindsey Vonn and singer Taylor Swift. The two were once seen having dinner together at a restaurant. The television reality series *The Bachelor* suggested it might invite Tebow to be one of its next male stars. Constant speculation about Tebow's romantic relationships is another reason the quarterback remains in the spotlight, but aside from his revelation that he is saving himself for marriage, he remains notoriously quiet on the topic of romance.

Well-Known Weaknesses

Tebow's playing style makes football fun to watch, but his critics say it is not sustainable. Opposing coaches and teams watch film footage of Tebow's previous games to learn how he plays and predict what he might do in a given situation. Then they craft defensive plans to stop him. The longer Tebow plays in the NFL, the fewer surprises he may be able to pull off. He will have to learn to pass more efficiently if he is to enjoy a long and successful career. Never knowing what Tebow might do is exciting for fans but stressful for coaches, who would rather see their teams have a solid lead throughout a game instead of relying on a miracle in the final moments. With Tebow, every game is a gamble. Coaches, like fans and teammates, tend to feel frustrated when players give inconsistent performances, since a team that loses too many games could cost a coach his job. Taking a chance and playing Tebow often pays off, but most coaches prefer whole-game reliability over last-minute power plays.

Tebow was traded to the New York Jets in 2012. He generated a lot of excitement and enthusiasm for the football program, even though his football skills were inconsistant.

Tebow's lack of consistency was hyped as a big reason why Denver Broncos coach John Fox traded him to the New York Jets in early 2012. In exchange the Broncos got starting quarterback Peyton Manning, a four-time NFL most valuable player (MVP) and a former Super Bowl MVP. He is regarded as one of the best and most consistent quarterbacks of all time. Trading Tebow for Manning secured a more seasoned and reliable quarterback for the Broncos, heading off the possibility that Tebow might have performed poorly in future seasons with the Broncos.

Tebow's trade to his new team brought out Jets fans in droves, and the new Jets jerseys with Tebow's name on them were among the hottest-selling items in the NFL in the spring of 2012. "For good reason, Tim has always had a great following," says Fox. "A player and person like Tim doesn't come around very often."[38]

Athletic Evangelism

While Tebow has many fans, some of his most ardent followers are not especially fans of football, but of Christianity. An outspoken evangelical Christian, Tebow wears his spiritual beliefs on his sleeve—literally. He writes Bible verses on his forearm pad, replacing the inscriptions he so famously wore on the black adhesive patches beneath his eyes when he was in college. He kneels on the sidelines and even in the end zone to pray during and after important parts of games, a practice now so well-known that it has spawned a new verb in popular culture—*Tebowing*, defined as getting down on one knee and praying. Tebow also points to the sky and gazes heavenward when things go his way in a game. He attends church. He ends all of his speeches and press conferences with the words "God bless."

Christians by the millions admire Tebow's public displays of values they share, but others are put off by it. Many critics claim that sports and religion are two distinct arenas, and football fans should not be subjected to watching Tebow pray on the field

Very religious and spirtual, Tebow is known for taking a knee and praying at football games. This action has become a cultural phenomenon, and actually has an official word associated with it: Tebowing.

or to listening to him invoke the Lord's name in his after-game press conferences. Football, they say, is not the right venue to push one's religion. "Tim Tebow is admirably inspired by his strong faith," writes sports journalist Diana Nyad, "but when he wears a uniform, he owes that team the respect of making his faith more private expression, less public spectacle."[39] Many people whose religion differs from Tebow's or who are not religious at all find his acts of piety inappropriate, at least while he is on the field.

Tebow's admirers, however, often cite his religiosity as a refreshing change in a popular culture that more often seems to shun religion. Even at his most spiritual, they say, Tebow gives protesters little to be upset about. "He's mostly show and no tell," writes sports columnist Sally Jenkins. "His idea of proselytizing is to tweet an abbreviated Bible citation. Mark 8:36. He leaves it up to you whether to look it up."[40] As for his habit of kneeling, Tebow is not the only athlete to display his religious beliefs vocally and visibly. At least since 1964, when boxing champion Cassius Clay changed his name to Muhammad Ali to reflect his Islamic beliefs, displays of religion have been common in professional sports. Baseball player Adrian Gonzalez swings a bat with a Bible verse etched into it. Basketball player Dwight Howard told reporters that a playoff victory proved God was present in his life. Tebow's praying in public, therefore, is not unheard of for an athlete. "On the whole, it's more restrained than most end-zone shimmies,"[41] according to Jenkins.

Whether people interpret it as admirable or inappropriate, Tebow's faith displays have created a spectrum of admirers and critics. Patton Dodd, the author of *The Tebow Mystique: The Faith and Fans of Football's Most Polarizing Player*, writes, "Your feelings about Tim can be seen as a litmus test of your political and social identity. You think he's bound to be a winner in spite of his unproven ability? You may be a naïve evangelical. You're questioning his chances as an NFL quarterback? You must hate people who love Jesus."[42] Dodd's sarcastic statement shows how Tebow admirers and Tebow critics often seem to view each other: Critics see the admirers as ridiculous for believing Tebow is a religious icon, and the admirers see the critics as opposed to Christianity altogether.

Laws in Tebow's Name

A successful product of homeschooling, Tebow has been linked to a public push across the United States for laws that would allow students who are homeschooled to take part in sports programs at public schools. The state of Florida allowed Tebow to play for the public high school of his choice, and that helped him to eventually become a professional football player. Without the exposure he gained playing football for a public high school, Tebow likely would not have had the interest of so many college recruiters and might not have attended the University of Florida. His successful entry into the NFL might never have

Country Crooner

Tim Tebow is a fan of country music, and country musicians seem to be fans of Tim Tebow. While still in college, Tebow and some teammates attended a Kenny Chesney concert, and the singer invited the quarterback onstage. Tebow sang along as Chesney sang "She Thinks My Tractor's Sexy." The crowd went wild.

In 2012 another country superstar, Brad Paisley, invited Tebow onstage with him. This time Tebow sang along with Paisley to "I'm Still a Guy." He received a standing ovation from the crowd and a Tebowing demonstration from Paisley.

occurred. Homeschool supporters in many states call for giving the 2 million homeschooled students in the United States the chance to participate in their local public schools' teams the way Tebow did.

Numerous states have passed laws that make public schools' extracurricular activities available to students who get their education at home. These pieces of legislation are popularly known as "Tebow laws." Twenty-nine states currently have laws that allow some homeschoolers to take part in some activities at public schools, and thirteen states allow widespread access. In 2012, the same year Tebow led the Broncos to their surprising playoff win, Virginia was one state considering laws that would allow homeschoolers access to team sports in its public schools. "A Tim Tebow law . . . I would support that," Virginia governor Bob McDonnell said at the time. "Home-school parents pay taxes like everybody else. It's just fair."[43] (Virginia's legislature did not end up passing the law, despite McDonnell's endorsement.)

Advocates for Tebow laws say that with proper restrictions, such laws will create valuable opportunities for sports participation to homeschooled students. They often use Tebow's success—both athletically and academically—as an example of what school teams could be missing out on by denying home-schoolers the opportunity to participate. "[Tebow's] example shows how this can work," says Robert Bell, a Virginia state legislator who championed the Tebow law. "You can do this successfully, it doesn't tear down other athletics, it doesn't impede other students from being successful."[44]

Not everyone agrees that homeschoolers should participate in sports and other activities at public schools, however. Public-school students, parents, and community members who oppose Tebow laws argue that despite Tebow's success, sports and other extracurricular activities are a privilege for students who attend the school, not a right of every child who lives in the area. Even though homeschoolers have to try out for teams just like the enrolled students, critics express concern that enrolled students will be excluded from playing if homeschooled students beat them out of spots on the team. "If my football team is so good that you want to come and participate on my football team, what's wrong with my chemistry class, what's wrong with my algebra class?"[45] asks Susan Bechtol of the Virginia High School League, a nonprofit organization that conducts programs for the public high schools in Virginia. She points out that public schools are quality programs for more than just their sports, and it seems hypocritical for homeschoolers to expect to be allotted space in a school's successful extracurricular programs when those students are unwilling to spend any time in the school's academic setting.

Those who oppose Tebow laws also worry that students who study at home may not face the same strict requirements for grades and academic eligibility as public school students—most schools have a minimum grade point average (GPA) athletes must maintain in order to play sports, whereas a homeschooled student's GPA might not be determined by the school's same rigorous standards. Critics also point out that public schools receive funding based on how many students are enrolled in the school; it would be unfair, they say, to let homeschooled students participate in a school's programs if the school does not receive funds for those students, because it is the school that pays for the programs.

Since Tebow is the namesake for such legislation, the debate has made him unpopular in some sectors of society. The debate is complicated, however. Not all homeschooled families are in favor of Tebow laws, and not all public-school families are against them, either. Still, the debate over homeschoolers and public school extracurricular activities have brought Tebow's name into the conversation.

Tebow and Abortion

Tebow has also been involved in another public debate, this one more politically charged than any other. Before he was drafted into the NFL, Tebow and his mother, Pam, appeared in a commercial sponsored by Focus on the Family, a conservative, pro-life Christian organization. For most of the commercial the camera focuses on Pam as she talks about her difficult pregnancy with her youngest child. At the end of the spot, Tebow dives into the scene, playfully tackling his mother. The commercial never mentions the word *abortion*, but it implies that if Pam had listened to the advice to terminate her pregnancy, the world would never have known Tim Tebow. "It's not a political ad, it's an inspiring family story at a time when people need to hear and see those stories,"[46] says Focus on the Family spokesperson Gary Schneeberger. Many people, however, consider the ad to be an antiabortion statement.

Few issues in America are as politically charged as abortion. Despite the landmark Supreme Court decision in the *Roe v. Wade* court case in 1974 that made abortion legal throughout the United States, the debate continues. Some people believe that a woman should have the right to choose whether or not to have an abortion. They believe that a woman and her doctor are the best people to be making medical decisions for her and that the government should not be involved. Other people believe that human life begins the moment a woman becomes pregnant and that abortion is murder.

With his commercial, first aired during the 2010 Super Bowl, Tebow made both allies and enemies by taking a side in this

A Well-Known Celebrity

Seventy-five percent of Americans know who Tim Tebow is. His celebrity rivals that of talk-show host Oprah Winfrey, singers Adele and Justin Bieber, and actor Brad Pitt. Forty-three percent of respondents in a nationwide Poll Position survey in 2012 said they believe Tebow wins games by divine intervention.

To help welcome the newly drafted New York Jet Quarterback to the Big Apple, Jockey showed their support with a huge billboard.

He is equal parts football persona and icon of modern Christianity. Although much of the press he receives is critical about his values and his skills, the negative hype only adds to his fame.

highly charged debate. Many fans rallied behind him, while many others disapproved of his moralizing. Even some who took no position in the abortion debate claimed they did not want to see a commercial about it in the middle of America's best-loved and most-watched sporting event of the year. Still others admired Tebow for standing up for his beliefs in front of millions of viewers, whether they agreed with him or not. "I think they [viewers] can at least respect that I stand up for what I believe, and I'm never shy about that," he says. "I don't feel like I'm very preachy about it, but I do stand up for what I believe."[47] Others, however, thought Tebow had inappropriately involved himself in a subject that has nothing to do with football. "This Super Bowl commercial represents a new strategy," writes journalist Jason Fagone, "one that's more confrontational and also much more in keeping with the family's ultraconservative roots."[48]

All Eyes on Tebow

Tebow rarely shares details of his private life unless he is asked. He surprised much of America, for example, when he announced at a 2009 press conference that he was still a virgin in response to a reporter's question about whether he was saving himself for marriage. Tebow expressed surprise at being asked such a personal question. "I didn't understand—and still don't—why it was something that needed to be asked," he writes in *Through My Eyes*. "Since when does anyone else get asked that?"[49]

In March 2012, Tebow held a press conference as a new member of the New York Jets. Even though Tebow would be the second string quarterback, there was so much media interest, the location had to be moved to the team's training center.

Some think Tebow's high-profile is not the result of him flaunting his views but rather the reality of living under neverending media scrutiny. For example, Tebow was not the only college football player who ever inscribed messages on his eye black, but his inscriptions were noticed by millions of Americans because news cameras were constantly taking close-ups of his face. "We see him praying on the sidelines a lot these days, but much of the reason is that our cameras are trained on him," Dodd writes. "Tebow isn't doing anything much different from a lot of other religious players. He's just doing it in the limelight."[50]

Tebow admits he uses his fame as a platform for influencing others, but that influence has had a positive impact on many lives. Even under the constant watch of reporters, Tebow has a reputation as a Good Samaritan. "He's genuine," says Stewart McHie, an expert on brand development and management, giving his own explanation for Tebow's popularity. "I don't think you could find a disingenuous bone in his body. He just makes you feel good."[51]

Chapter 5

Life Off the Field

In his private life Tim Tebow pursues quieter goals and gives his time and money to helping others. "Tim Tebow . . . is almost unnaturally polite and humble, living an exceedingly philanthropic life while encouraging others to do the same," writes journalist and blogger William Sullivan. "He seems to make the most of his opportunities to give others personal joy."[52]

Giving Back

During his years at the University of Florida, Tebow was not only well respected on campus but also in the surrounding community. Beginning in his freshman year, he used his limited free time to make public appearances. He visited prisons to speak to inmates. He went to hospitals to spend time with sick children, many of whom had life-threatening diseases. He rallied other Florida football players to do the same. "I don't know if Florida was real heavy on all the charity work until he came,"[53] says Ryan Stamper, former Florida linebacker and Tebow's college teammate.

During spring and summer breaks, when most other players took vacations, Tebow spent his free time traveling with his father and his older brothers to the Philippines. There he gave speeches about faith and Christianity. He also worked to inspire and encourage his audiences, especially kids who attended poor schools. Tebow frequently visited hospitals and orphanages; his favorite was Uncle Dick's Home, an orphanage started by a close family friend of the Tebows. It remains one of many causes the quarterback supports. "The unselfishness of his mission outside of college football is unparalleled," said Florida coach Urban Meyer

A W15H Come True

The Tim Tebow Foundation's W15H program (the word *WISH*, with Tebow's jersey number standing in for the *I* and *S*) brought many deserving guests to Broncos games during the 2011 season. One of the most memorable was twenty-year-old Zack McLeod. A former football star at a private New England high school, McLeod dreamed of a college football scholarship and perhaps a career like Tebow's, but in 2008, that dream ended when he suffered a traumatic and nearly fatal brain injury during a game. McLeod's injury caused permanent disabilities, including limited speech.

Tebow invited McLeod to the 2011 NFL play-off game between the Broncos and the Patriots. He passed him a ball, demonstrating a special kinship with the young man.

in 2009. "I don't know if there will ever be another one like him. . . . He's the best ambassador I've ever seen of college football."[54]

Changing the Game for the Needy

During Tebow's sophomore year at Florida, he decided to do more than visit hospitals and prisons. He also wanted to raise money for causes he thought important. Colleges and universities have strict rules about how athletes can raise money and what they can use it for, but Tebow found a way to make his ideas a reality. He teamed up with student government and fourteen campus sororities to sponsor a sorority flag football tournament called First and 15 in the spring of 2008. The event raised about ten thousand dollars for Uncle Dick's Home and to build a playroom for the Shands Hospital for Children at the University of Florida in Gainesville, Florida. "Tim did a fantastic job," said Ryan Moseley, former student body president who helped make First and 15 happen. "For a guy to have a schedule like that and pull this off—that's true credit to him."[55]

Working with sick children and orphans is one of Tebow's passions. Here, he plays football with one of his youngest fans, Preston Winslow, who is undergoing treatment for Acute myeloid leukemia.

First and 15 was so popular that Tebow and others at the university repeated it the following year. They also expanded it into a weeklong event and opened participation to all women's groups on campus. Gators football players coached the sororities, and the week had multiple events, including a draft for coaches and a five-hundred-guest banquet. More than a hundred volunteers took part in the effort. The 2009 First and 15 raised almost $340,000, more than any student-sponsored fundraising activity had ever collected in the United States.

In addition to helping orphans and local pediatric patients, First and 15 volunteers also identified ten underprivileged kids from the community to take on a day trip to Disney World. Tebow and other players accompanied the kids for the whole day and gave them Gator jerseys and gifts. None of the kids had been to the theme park before, and two had endured the death of their father just weeks before the trip. Coach Meyer says,

> Tim has made community service and commitment to serving others a cool thing among his peers. He has changed the way kids his age look at helping others. He has made it O.K. to volunteer and give back. He has given people beyond his peer group permission to speak up for what they believe in. He has made all of us evaluate a sense of higher calling in what we do every day.[56]

New Arena, Same Ideals

After he graduated from college in 2010, Tebow, freed from the NCAA's fund-raising restrictions, started his own foundation, the Tim Tebow Foundation, to raise money for his favorite causes. Partly as an offshoot of First and 15, the foundation partners with the Dreams Come True program of Jacksonville, Florida, and other national wish-granting organizations to fulfill the wishes of kids with life-threatening illnesses whose wish is to meet Tim Tebow. The foundation also partners with CURE International, a nonprofit organization that is the largest provider of reconstructive surgery for children in the world, to raise money to build a hospital in the Philippines that will specialize in treating children with physical handicaps or deformities that are correctable with surgery. In February 2012 construction began on the Tebow CURE Hospital, a thirty-bed surgical facility that will provide surgeries for children with crippling conditions such as disfigured spines or clubfoot. About one-third of these surgeries will be performed for free for those families that cannot afford treatment. The hospital is scheduled to open in early 2014.

Tebow also intends to bring a Timmy's Playroom, like the one at the Shands Hospital for Children in Gainesville, to the Tebow CURE Hospital. When completed, it will be the first international hospital playroom of its kind. "We feel blessed that the Tim Tebow Foundation has chosen to partner with us to bring

One Day with Tebow

In April 2012, during the second annual Tim Tebow Foundation Celebrity Golf Tournament, two anonymous individuals made big news. At a live auction during the event, the unnamed guests bid $100,000 to spend one day with Tebow. The money benefited the foundation's charity work, but what Tebow had to do in exchange was better still—the donors simply wanted him to visit underprivileged kids in a Florida neighborhood. They even offered to pay for Tebow's airfare, in addition to the cash gift to his foundation. "It was very humbling," says Tebow. "That day I feel like I've got to do a few extra things to be special, you know? I've got to try to be a little better."

Quoted in *Florida Today.* "Couple Donates $100K to Spend Day with Tim Tebow, Underprivileged Children," April 15, 2012.

first-world quality care and spiritual healing to the children of the Philippines,"[57] says Scott Harrison, founder and president of CURE International.

To help raise money for the hospital, the Tim Tebow Foundation launched a Dollar Day campaign in November 2011. It asked all Tebow fans to give just one dollar each with the goal of raising, in a single day, the $700,000 that was still needed to make the Tebow CURE Hospital a reality. The effort fell short of its goal by about a $100,000.

The Tim Tebow Foundation also contributes money to Uncle Dick's Home, the orphanage for which Tebow originally raised money with his First and 15 events. The Christian-based home provides education, transportation, clothing, food, housing, and medical needs for as many as fifty children whose families are unable to care for them. The Tim Tebow Foundation has a goal that 100 percent of every dollar donated to it goes to help causes like Uncle Dick's Home, a rare ambition even for a nonprofit organization.

In Jacksonville, Florida, Tebow speaks at the opening of his foundations first Timmy's Playroom.

Person to Person

Tebow's fame lets him organize and publicize fund-raising and charity programs on a grand scale. Perhaps where his goodwill shines through the most, however, is in the way he relates to average people. A good example is the 2009 Home Depot ESPNU College Football Awards ceremony at Disney World. The night before the show, Tebow met twenty-year-old Kelly Faughnan, who a year earlier had undergone surgery for a brain tumor that left her with hearing loss and a noticeable, continuous tremor. During her recovery, Faughnan told her family she wanted to go to Disney World and see Tebow at the awards ceremony. When Tebow heard that Faughnan was outside the ESPN Zone restaurant and wanted to meet him, he invited her inside and sat with her at dinner. Later in the evening he asked her to be his date for the awards ceremony the following night. He and Faughnan have kept in touch ever since.

Tebow also works with his foundation to find someone to be his special guest at each of his professional games. The guest,

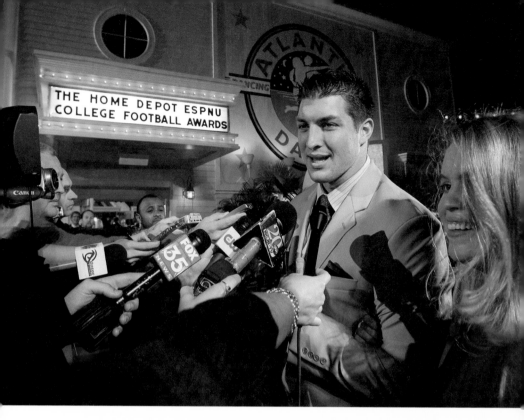

Brain tumor survivor and Tim Tebow fan Kelly Faughnan accompanies the quarterback on the red carpet of the 2009 ESPNU College Football Awards. Tebow invited the fan to be his date for the high-profile event. They have kept in touch ever since.

usually a child or teenager with a serious illness or disability, and a few of their family members receive complimentary airfare to the game. They attend pregame activities, watch the game, and spend time with Tebow. His foundation treats them to dinner, pays for their stay at a nice hotel, and even sends them home with souvenirs that include a Bible, luggage, and an autographed Tebow football card.

After he was traded to the New York Jets, Tebow continued hosting one guest per week. Guests for Tebow's 2012 Jets season included a teenager with brain and spinal cancer and another with cerebral palsy. About three hundred people, including dozens of wish-granting organizations, contact the Tim Tebow Foundation each year to refer a child for the program. The organization carefully considers all the referrals before choosing the fifteen children and teens to include in the program for the season. The foundation actively raises funds to pay for the program, about $125,000 per year. Tebow's popularity and goodwill draw tens of thousands of dollars in donations to the program annually.

Fully invested in the wish-granting program, Tebow regularly forgoes postgame celebrations to spend time with his special guests; many people are not aware of the time Tebow devotes to his weekly guests of honor. The quarterback claims these moments are more meaningful to him than whatever happens during a football game. "I can take off my helmet, run over there and spend a few moments with someone who is dealing with so much more than I've ever had to deal with," he says."[58]

Going for the Green

Tebow is always thinking of ways to use his fame to help people, and during the off-season, he and his foundation organize the Tim Tebow Foundation Celebrity Golf Classic. His 2012 tournament brought together famous athletes, such as football player and Heisman Trophy winner Danny Wuerffel and Olympic champion skier Lindsey Vonn, as well as singer Jordin Sparks and the country music group Rascal Flatts. Attendees pay to watch the tournament and interact with the celebrities, with all the proceeds going to Tebow's chosen charities.

Also present at the 2012 tournament was professional golfer Bubba Watson. He admits that for a long time he did not like Tebow, who in college led the Florida Gators to wins against Watson's favorite college team, the University of Georgia Bulldogs. "He kept making these incredible jump passes and doing so many other things to beat us," Watson says. "I didn't like him much back then. Not at all, really." The golfer has since changed his opinion of the quarterback, however, and when Tebow invited him to take part in the 2012 tournament, he readily agreed. "I respect him as a person and what he stands for," he says. "You can be inspired by Tim just by watching him play football and what he does away from the football for charity, for his church."[59]

Tebow's Private Life

Tebow does not spend all of his time playing football and doing charity work. Like everyone else, he has hobbies and favorite pastimes, like golfing and spending time with his family. Unlike many professional athletes, Tebow does not go to nightclubs or party, and he says he never drinks because he is mindful that he is a role model. "The biggest reason I don't (consume alcohol)," he says in an interview with the newspaper *USA Today*, "is because (if I have) a glass of wine, I don't want to be responsible for a kid looking up to me and saying, 'Hey, Tebow's doin' it—I am going to do it.'"[60]

Tebow says he likes to spend his free time with his close-knit family and with good friends. As for food, he likes steak and potatoes and ice cream—vanilla—which he only allows himself to eat about once a week because he sticks to a strict diet for his athletic training. When he is home in Jacksonville, Florida, he attends the First Baptist Church. During football season, it difficult for Tebow to choose a place of worship:

Golfer Bubba Watson was not a fan of Tebow's when he played for University of Florida. However, Tebow's charitable work changed Watson's opinion and the two athletes now share mutual respect and friendship.

Tebow for President

In a poll of about twenty-five hundred American voters taken right before the 2012 Super Bowl, Tebow beat out all other current NFL quarterbacks as the best fit to be president of the United States someday. Tebow himself has said he would not rule out a stint in politics at some point in the future, perhaps after retiring from his NFL career. He cannot be president until he is at least thirty-five years old, the required minimum age. President Tebow may be a stretch, but the quarterback could have a future as a senator, congressman, or governor. He would not be the first athlete or celebrity to end up in politics, and his proven fund-raising ability and popularity could make him a formidable opponent in any election.

There are hundreds of churches to choose from in New York. But the New York Jets has a team chaplain who conducts Saturday-night services while the players are on the road or busy with game preparations on Sunday mornings during the football season. Tebow's presence also sometimes brings church to him. When he spoke at an outdoor Easter Sunday service in Georgetown, Texas, in 2012, for example, Tebow drew a crowd of fifteen thousand people. Tebow's presence seems to draw out those of the Christian faith, and some people joke that because of Tebow's on-field displays of faith, Sunday NFL games have become a mix of football and church.

Public Perception

While many professional athletes are rich, famous, and easily recognizable by the public, they are also human beings who sometimes engage in unacceptable behavior, even illegal activities. This can jeopardize their career and alienate their fans. In December 2012, Dallas Cowboys linebacker Josh Brent was charged with manslaughter when, while driving under the influence of alcohol, he crashed his vehicle, which resulted in the death of his passenger and teammate Jerry Brown. A week before that accident occurred, Jovan Belcher, a linebacker for the Kansas City Chiefs, shot and killed his girlfriend, and then himself.

Golf prodigy Tiger Woods is another athlete who saw his reputation plummet when the public learned he was cheating on his wife with several women over the course of their relationship. In the wake of the revelation, the divorce from his wife, and the widespread public disapproval, Woods performed poorly on the golf course. Many other professional athletes with big reputations have fallen from grace in similar ways, such as abusing drugs or alcohol, getting in trouble with the law, or engaging in other unacceptable behavior.

So far, Tebow has not made any missteps and still enjoys the respect of his fans. ESPN sports contributor Melissa Jacobs calls him "a rarity in a league whose superstars are often mired in scandal."[61] In an era in which fans worship professional athletes, Tebow's fan base has been stronger and larger than most. He is widely admired for his character, piety, and commitment to his ideals. The hype over Tebow also means he is scrutinized closely. Those who dislike the quarterback watch and wait for him to make a career-killing mistake or reveal a character vice. Only time will tell if Tebow will fall from grace. "If you believe, unbelievable things can sometimes be possible,"[62] he says.

Chapter 1: Growing Up Gifted

1. Quoted in Michelle Stuckey. "Pam Tebow Tells of Keeping Faith Through Tough Times." *Gainesville (FL) Sun*, May 17, 2009. www.gainesville.com/article/20090517/articles/90517101.

2. Quoted in Stuckey. "Pam Tebow Tells of Keeping Faith Through Tough Times."

3. Quoted in "Tim Tebow 'Focus on the Family' Super Bowl Commercial Video." Book Room Reviews, February 7, 2010. www.bookroomreviews.com/2010/02/07/tim-tebow-focus-on-the-family-super-bowl-commercial-video/.

4. Quoted in Mike Klis. "'Will to Win:' Excerpts from the Denver Post's Chronicle of Tim Tebow and the 2011 Broncos." *Denver Post*, January 23, 2012. www.denverpost.com/broncos/ci_19790554#ixzz27KlRNtAi.

5. Tim Tebow. *Through My Eyes*, with Nathan Whitaker. New York: HarperCollins, 2011, pp. 10, 12.

6. Tebow. *Through My Eyes*, p. 12.

7. Dave Curtis. "Tebow Caused Stir Even as a Youngster." *Orlando Sentinel*, December 5, 2007. http://articles.orlandosentinel.com/2007-12-05/sports/tebowthekid05_1_quarterback-tim-tebow-hess-allen.

8. Quoted in Curtis. "Tebow Caused Stir Even as Youngster."

9. Quoted in Robbie Andreu. "Team Tebow." *Gainesville (FL) Sun*, January 31, 2006. www.gainesville.com/article/20060131/GATORS01/201310351?p=1&tc=pg.

10. Quoted in Andreu. "Team Tebow."

11. Quoted in Justin Barney. "Nease Teammates, Coach Say They Knew Tim Tebow Would Achieve Current Status." Jacksonville.com, January 13, 2012. http://m.jacksonville.com/sports/college/florida-gators/2012-01-13/story/nease-teammates-coach-say-they-knew-tim-tebow-would.

12. Quoted in Barney. "Nease Teammates, Coach Say They Knew Tim Tebow Would Achieve Current Status."

Chapter 2: Into the Gator Swamp

13. Clarence K. Moniba. *The Official Guidebook to a College Football Scholarship.* Bloomington, IN: Xlibris, 2001, p. 19.

14. Quoted in Henry Gola. "Tim Tebow Commits to Florida." ESPN Insider, December 13, 2005. http://insider.espn .go.com/ncaa/recruiting/news/story?id=2257886&action=l ogin&appRedirect=http%3a%2f%2finsider.espn.go.com%2 fncaa%2frecruiting%2fnews%2fstory%3fid%3d2257886.

15. Quoted in Chase Goodbread. "Florida? Alabama? Tebow to Choose." *Florida Times-Union.* December 13, 2005. http:// jacksonville.com/tu-online/stories/121305/hig_20548757 .shtml.

16. Quoted in "Athlon Archive: The Totally True Tales of Tim Tebow." Athlon Sports, August 22, 2011. www.athlonsports .com/college-football/athlon-archive-totally-true-tales-tim-tebow.

17. Jim Donnan. "Florida vs. Ohio State: ESPN's Take." ESPN. com, January 8, 2007. http://sports.espn.go.com/ncf/ bowls06/index.

18. Quoted in "Then and Now: Tim Tebow's Journey." CBS Denver, January 12, 2012. http://denver.cbslocal .com/2012/01/12/then-and-now-tim-tebows-journey/.

19. Quoted in Antonya English. "Meyer: Tebow Limited by Shoulder Injury." *St. Petersburg Times*, October 29, 2007. http://news.google.com/newspapers?nid=888&dat=2007 1029&id=QvNRAAAAIBAJ&sjid=tHQDAAAAIBAJ&pg= 2417,3828441.

20. Quoted in Mike Bianchi. "If Tebow Beats Alabama, I Say He'll Win Heisman." *Orlando (FL) Sentinel*, December 1, 2008. http://blogs.orlandosentinel.com/sports_bianchi /2008/12/if-tebow-beats.html.

21. Phil. 4:13 (New American Standard Version). Biblos.com. http://bible.cc/philippians/4-13.htm.

22. Quoted in "Tebow 'Promise' Speech Now Memorialized." NBC Sports, March 18, 2009. http://collegefootballtalk .nbcsports.com/2009/03/18/tebow-promise-speech-now-memorialized/.

23. John 3:16 (New American Standard Version). Biblos.com. http://bible.cc/john/3-16.htm.
24. Quoted in "Tebow Speech Engraved on Plaque." ESPN.com, March 25, 2009. http://sports.espn.go.com/ncf/news/story?id=4016429.
25. Tebow. *Through My Eyes*, p. 226.

Chapter 3: Going Pro

26. Quoted in John Walters. "Tim Tebow Talk Puts Todd McShay's Reputation on the Line." AOL News, January 29, 2010. www.aolnews.com/2010/01/29/tim-tebow-talk-puts-todd-mcshays-reputation-on-the-line/.
27. Quoted in Andy Staples. "Florida's Pro Day Was a True Circus, with Tim Tebow Front and Center." SI.com, March 17, 2010. http://sportsillustrated.cnn.com/2010/writers/andy_staples/03/17/tim.tebow.pro.day/index.html#ixzz1snSOTEnJ.
28. Keet Bailey. "2010 NFL Draft: Top 10 Hardest Players to Place." NFL Soup, February 21, 2010. http://nflsoup.com/?p=1904.
29. Quoted in David Jones. "Tim Tebow Headed to Broncos After Big Surprise in NFL Draft." *USA Today*, April 23, 2010. www.usatoday.com/sports/football/nfl/broncos/2010-04-22-tim-tebow_N.htm.
30. Quoted in "What They Said: Broncos Inspired After Halftime vs. Houston." *Denver Post*, December 26, 2010. www.denverpost.com/broncos/ci_16947462#ixzz1ssHisBRs.
31. Quoted in Judy Battista. "Tebow, Imperfect but Captivating, Makes His Case." *New York Times*, December 27, 2010. www.nytimes.com/2010/12/28/sports/football/28fastforward.html?pagewanted=all.
32. Quoted in Kenny Legan. "2011 Season Review: Second Quarter." DenverBroncos.com, January 31, 2012. www.denverbroncos.com/news-and-blogs/article-1/2011-Season-Review-Second-Quarter/7511fe06-b712-44dc-9f4e-ee6ee9a186d1.

33. Quoted in Legan. "2011 Season Review."

34. Jamison Hensley. "Steelers Lost by Underestimating Tebow." ESPN.com, January 8, 2012. http://espn.go.com/blog/afcnorth/post/_/id/39998/steelers-lost-by-underestimating-tebow.

35. Quoted in Monty. "John Elway and John Fox Statements on Tim Tebow." BroncoTalk, March 21, 2012. http://broncotalk.net/2012/03/32258/broncos-blog/john-elway-and-john-fox-statements-on-tim-tebow/.

Chapter 4: A Controversial Career

36. Ryan Klocke. "Tim Tebow the Pop Culture Icon: He's Succeeded Where So Many Athletes Failed." Bleacher Report, January 11, 2012. http://bleacherreport.com/articles/1020262-tim-tebow-the-pop-culture-icon-hes-succeeded-where-so-many-athletes-failed.

37. Quoted in "TebowMania: Afflicted or Impervious?" ESPNW, December 14, 2011. http://espn.go.com/espnw/commentary/7353209/getting-caught-tim-tebow-craze.

38. Quoted in Mike Florio. "Broncos Announce Tebow Trade." ProFootballTalk.com, March 21, 2012. http://profootballtalk.nbcsports.com/2012/03/21/broncos-announce-tebow-trade/.

39. Diana Nyad. "Tim Tebow: Separation of Church and Sport." Huffington Post, January 27, 2012. www.huffingtonpost.com/diana-nyad/tim-tebow-religion-sports_b_1236698.html.

40. Sally Jenkins. "Bill Maher and Tim Tebow: Why Are So So Many Offended by the Quarterback's Faith?" *Washington Post*, December 30, 2011. www.washingtonpost.com/sports/bill-maher-and-tim-tebow-why-are-so-so-many-offended-by-the-quarterbacks-faith/2011/12/30/gIQACSudQP_story.html.

41. Jenkins. "Bill Maher and Tim Tebow."

42. Patton Dodd. *The Tebow Mystique: The Faith and Fans of Football's Most Polarizing Player*. Englewood, CO: Patheos Press, 2011. Kindle edition.

43. Quoted in Laura Vozzella. "Va. Gov. McDonnell Supports 'Tebow Law.'" *Washington Post*, January 10, 2012. www .washingtonpost.com/blogs/virginia-politics/post/va-gov-mcdonnell-supports-tebow-law/2012/01/10/gIQA3wB-BoP_blog.html.

44. Quoted in Tyler James. "Homeschoolers Invoke 'Tebow' to Play Public Sports." CBN News, February 19, 2012. www .cbn.com/cbnnews/us/2012/February/Homeschoolers-Invoke-Tebow-to-Play-Public-Sports/.

45. Quoted in James. "Homeschoolers Invoke 'Tebow to Play Public Sports.'"

46. Quoted in "Tebow's Pro-life Ad Set for Super Bowl." *Washington Times*, January 26, 2010. www.washingtontimes .com/news/2010/jan/26/tebows-pro-life-ad-set-for-super-bowl/?page=all.

47. Quoted in "Tebow's Pro-life Ad Set for Super Bowl."

48. Jason Fagone. "Tim Tebow Goes for the Conversion: The Real Meaning of the Quarterback's Pro-Life Super Bowl Ad." *Slate*, January 29, 2010. www.slate.com/articles/sports/ sports_nut/2010/01/tim_tebow_goes_for_the_conversion .html.

49. Tebow. *Through My Eyes*, p. 214.

50. Dodd. *The Tebow Mystique*, Kindle edition.

51. Quoted in Tim Rasmussen. "Tim Tebow Stands at Crossroads of Sports, Religion and Popular Culture." *Washington Post*, December 9, 2011. www.washingtonpost.com/sports/redskins /tim-tebow-stands-at-the-apex-of-sports-religion-and-popular-culture/2011/12/09/gIQA8iHWlO_story_1.html.

Chapter 5: Life Off the Field

52. William Sullivan. "The Magic of the Tim Tebow Saga." American Thinker, December 18, 2011. www.americanthinker .com/2011/12/the_magic_of_the_tim_tebow_saga.html.

53. Quoted in Ben Volin. "Tim Tebow: A Historic Career Enters the Final Stretch." *Atlanta Journal-Constitution*, November 30, 2009. www.ajc.com/sports/tim-tebow-a-historic-219513 .html.

54. Quoted in Volin. "Tim Tebow."
55. Quoted in Stephanie Rosenberg. "Sorority Members Pass Pigskin for First and 15 Charity Game." *Independent Florida Alligator*, April 14, 2008. www.alligator.org/news/campus/article_e2729d56-a52c-5947-a5af-12fe2c09a511.html.
56. Quoted in "What Others Say." Tim Tebow Foundation. www.timtebowfoundation.org/quotes.
57. Quoted in Cure International. "Tim Tebow Foundation, CURE International to Build Children's Hospital in Philippines." Press release, November 15, 2011. www.prnewswire.com/news-releases/tim-tebow-foundation-cure-international-to-build-childrens-hospital-in-philippines-133848603.html.
58. Quoted in Suzan Clarke. "Tim Tebow Says Football Comes After Faith and Family." *Good Morning America*, April 12, 2012. http://gma.yahoo.com/tim-tebow-says-football-comes-faith-family-031737467--abc-news-topstories.html.
59. Quoted in Steve DiMeglia. "Bubba's New (and Unlikely) Buddy: Tim Tebow." *USA Today*, September 3, 2012. www.usatoday.com/sports/football/nfl/story/2012-08-30/Bubbas-new-and-unlikely-buddy-Tim-Tebow/57561532/1.
60. Quoted in Jon Saraceno. "Tim Tebow: The Man Behind the Mania." *USA Today*, January 13, 2012. www.usatoday.com/sports/football/nfl/story/2012-01-11/tebow-exclusive/52518122/1.
61. Quoted in "TebowMania."
62. Quoted in Jon Greenberg. "Bears Get Tebowed." ESPN.com, December 12, 2011. http://espn.go.com/chicago/nfl/story/_/id/7343676/tim-tebow-leads-denver-broncos-comeback-win-chicago-bears.

1987

Timothy Richard Tebow is born on August 14 in Manila, Philippines.

1995

Tebow joins Pop Warner, youth football organization, in Jacksonville, Florida.

2001

Tebow starts playing high school football as an eighth grader.

2005

Nease High School wins the Florida state championship title with Tebow at quarterback; featured in *The Chosen One* documentary; Tebow commits to play for the University of Florida Gators.

2007

In January the Florida Gators, with Tebow on the team, wins the national championship; in September Tebow becomes starting quarterback for the Gators.

2008

Tebow receives the Maxwell Award for the College Player of the Year and the Davey O'Brien National Quarterback Award for best quarterback in the NCAA; he receives the Heisman Trophy, and is named an NCAA First-Team All American.

2009

The Gators win the national championship with Tebow as starting quarterback; Tebow's First and 15 event raises $340,000 for charity.

2010

In January Tebow plays his final game as a Florida Gator, breaking multiple conference records; he graduates from the University of Florida, and he starts the Tim Tebow Foundation. In April the Denver Broncos draft Tebow as the twenty-fifth pick of the first round of the NFL draft.

2012

The Denver Broncos trade Tebow to the New York Jets. In February construction began on the Tebow CURE hospital in the Philippines.

For More Information

Books

Mike Klis. *Will to Win: How Tim Tebow and the Denver Broncos Made 2011 a Season to Remember*. Denver, CO: Denver Post, 2012. The author of this book, a sports reporter for the *Denver Post* newspaper, recounts games and big moments in the 2011 Denver Broncos season, in which Tebow helped his team turn a losing season around and make an unforeseen showing at the playoffs.

Tim Tebow. *Through My Eyes*, with Nathan Whitaker. New York: HarperCollins, 2011. In his autobiography, Tebow tells the story of his birth, childhood, high school days, and the college football career that made him a star. He also discusses his faith, family relationships, and experiences on the football field.

Mike Yorkey. *Playing with Purpose: Inside the Lives and Faith of the NFL's Top New Quarterbacks—Sam Bradford, Colt McCoy, and Tim Tebow*. Saratoga, CA: Barbour Books, 2010. This book offers a comparison of the strong religious beliefs and football talents of Tim Tebow and two of his fellow college quarterbacks, Colt McCoy and Sam Bradford.

Internet Sources

Steve DiMeglio. "Bubba's New (and Unlikely) Buddy: Tim Tebow." *USA Today*, September 3, 2012. www.usatoday.com/sports/football/nfl/story/2012-08-30/Bubbas-new-and-unlikely-buddy-Tim-Tebow/57561532/1.

Patton Dodd. "Tim Tebow: God's Quarterback." *Wall Street Journal*, December 10, 2011. http://online.wsj.com/article/SB10001424052970203413304577084770973155282.html.

Nicholas Goss. "Tim Tebow: Why Bidding $100,000 to Spend Day with Jets Star Isn't Crazy." Bleacher Report, April 15, 2012. http://bleacherreport.com/articles/1146027-tim-tebow-why-bidding-100000-to-spend-day-with-jets-star-isnt-crazy.

Huffington Post. "Tim Tebow Foundation Raises More than $4 Million in First Year," July 27, 2012. www.huffington-post.com/2012/07/27/tim-tebow-foundation-fundraising_n_1710748.html.

Jon Meacham. "Tebow's Testimony." *Time*, January 16, 2012. www.time.com/time/magazine/article/0,9171,2103742-1,00.html.

Austin Murphy. "You Gotta Love Tim Tebow." *Sports Illustrated*, July 27, 2009. http://sportsillustrated.cnn.com/vault/article/magazine/MAG1158168/index.htm.

Seth Mydans. "A Father's Example Guides Tebow." *New York Times*, May 15, 2012. www.nytimes.com/2012/05/16/sports/football/for-tim-tebow-an-example-set-long-ago.html?pagewanted=all.

Rick Reilly. "I Believe in Tim Tebow." ESPN.com, January 13, 2012. http://espn.go.com/espn/story/_/id/7455943/believing-tim-tebow.

Jeff Schapiro. "Tim Tebow Foundation Program Continues to Bring Joy to Ailing Children." ChristianPost.com, August 23, 2012. www.christianpost.com/news/tim-tebow-foundation-program-continues-to-bring-joy-to-ailing-children-80443/.

Jim Trotter. "The Power of the Possible." *Sports Illustrated*, December 19, 2011. http://sportsillustrated.cnn.com/vault/article/magazine/MAG1193027/index.htm.

DVDs

Tim Tebow. *Tim Tebow: Everything in Between*. Directed by Chase Heavener. Eagan, MN: Summit Information, 2011.

This sixty-minute documentary follows Tim Tebow in 2010 during the four months between his college graduation and his draft into the NFL. It includes a look at his training regimen, commentary on his NFL chances, and discussions about his faith and work ethic.

Websites

NFL (www.nfl.com). This is the website of the National Football League. It offers information about games, teams, and players, including Tim Tebow.

Tim Tebow (www.timtebow.com). This is Tim Tebow's official website. It contains facts and statistics about him, photos, videos, and his upcoming game schedule. It also has links to his Facebook and Twitter feeds.

Tim Tebow Foundation (www.timtebowfoundation.org). This is the website for the Tim Tebow Foundation, a nonprofit organization that Tebow founded in 2010. The foundation raises money for the world's poorest children and grants wishes for kids with life-threatening illnesses.

Picture Credits

Cover: © Patrick Green/CSM/Landov
© Al Messerschmidt/Getty Images Sport, 29
© Andy Lyons/Getty Images Sport, 60
© AP Images/The Florida Times-Union, Kelly Jordan, 75
© Brandon Kruse/The Palm Beach Post/ZUMAPRESS.com/Newscom, 9
© Donald Miralle/Getty Images, 50
© Doug Benc/Getty Images Sport, 31, 76
© Doug Finger/Gainesville Sun/Landov, 16
© Doug Pensinger/Getty Images Sport, 45
© Ezra Shaw/Getty Images Sport, 62
© Gary C. Caskey/UPI/Newscom, 53
© Gary W. Green/Orlando Sentinel/MCT/Getty Images, 38
© Kelly Kline/Getty Images Sport, 22, 36
© Kevin Muzar/WireImage/Getty, 78
© Lexinton Herald-Leader/ZUMAPRESS/Newscom, 33, 41
© MCT via Getty Images, 14
© Mike Stobe/Getty Images Sport, 68
© NBCU Photo Bank via Getty Images, 10
© Octavio Jones/Tampa Bay Times/ZUMAPRESS/Newscom, 72
© Orlando Sentinel/MCT/Landov, 49
© Stephen Lovekin/Getty Images, 67
© Tom Hauck/Icon SMI 719/Newscom, 25, 27
© Tom Hertz/Alamy, 19

About the Author

Jenny MacKay is the author of more than fifteen nonfiction books for young readers on topics ranging from crime scene investigation to sports science. She lives in northern Nevada with her husband, son, and daughter, all of whom are big fans of the University of Nevada Wolf Pack football team.